DEDICATION

There are 8.29 million people in Sierra Leone, just over 4 million of whom are hardworking, resilient women. I dedicate this book to them. Each and every one of them.

Almost 50 per cent of Sierra Leonean women and girls endure "sexual or physical violence during their lifetime". This must stop. I am a Sierra Leonean woman, I was raised by strong, resilient Sierra Leonean women, and I know we are valuable contributors who are deserving of dignity and respect. Our women are resourceful cooks who make a little go a long way and waste nothing.

Sierra Leonean women, you are fierce, brave and strong. This book is dedicated to you.

KOLA NUTS (SEE IMAGE ON PREVIOUS PAGE)

Kola nuts, which grow on certain trees in the Cola genus native to West Africa, have been a treasured commodity and a powerful cultural symbol throughout West Africa for centuries. They are given as a gift to show respect and as a sacred offering. The nut is also incorporated into many rites of passage and used in ceremonies to cement treaties and contracts. These culturally significant, economically important, chestnut-size nuts have been carried far and wide and their therapeutic reputation has travelled with them over centuries and across continents. My beloved grandmother, Mariama Kabba, has been trading kola nuts for most of her life. Kola nut extract contains the stimulants caffeine, theobromine and kolatin along with glucose, and is able to counteract fatigue, alleviate thirst and hunger and may possibly enhance intellectual activity, as well as acting as a psychoactive substance and suppressing coughs. Kola nuts were used as currency and the trade has been part of my family history for generations.

MARIA BRADFORD

SWEET SALONE

RECIPES FROM
THE HEART OF
SIERRA LEONE

DESIGN & LOCATION PHOTOGRAPHY BY DAVE BROWN
RECIPE PHOTOGRAPHY BY YUKI SUGIURA

Hardie Grant

QUADRILLE

CONTENTS

INTRODUCTION

My name is Mariama. I was named after my grandmother, but for as long as I can remember everyone has called me Maria. Even my grandmother calls me Maria. I speak three languages – Krio, Mende and English – and I live in Kent with my family. I have many fond childhood memories of growing up in Freetown, the capital of Sierra Leone, all of which have influenced my recipes and the dishes I create. Food stories, food memories and my enduring love for the taste of home has taken me to this point. I have turned my lifelong passion of food into a fulfilling career.

I started my food business in 2017, creating delicious African food for dinner parties, weddings and corporate events. Back then, it was called Maria Bradford Kitchen, but my fellow Sierra Leoneans would describe my dishes as 'fancy'. They would say in Krio, *Dis na Shwen Shwen it*, which, in English, is an exclamation along the lines of, 'This is fancy food'. So, I decided to rename it what the people call it.

[Sh•wen Sh•wen] Adjective

Derived from the Krio language word for fancy.

I am really proud that Shwen Shwen is at the forefront of Sierra Leonean-inspired fine dining experiences. Africa is the final frontier of food, and whether we are using utensils or eating with our hands, our dishes can be prepared and consumed in a fine-dining environment. Dining etiquette in Africa's Atlantic Coast cultures may well be very different to that in Europe, but we too have our rules and traditions that go way back.

The first human settlements in West Africa date back to 4,000 BCE, and the roots of traditional Sierra Leonean food certainly reach this far too; many of the indigenous vegetables and spices that define our food – rice, yam, plantain, cassava and the like – all existed there thousands of years ago. The traditional dishes I cook (especially the plasas dishes, leafy green sauces) are all Sierra Leonean classics, and unapologetically time-consuming to prepare and cook.

I grew up in Freetown, a city that has a unique history and fascinating story when it comes to international trade. The fusion of culinary techniques and recipes has been in existence since the dawn of global travel. Initially, there was migration within Africa between different tribes, then Muslim traders brought Islam, and then Europeans and Lebanese arrived and returnees from London and the Caribbean, each bringing new experiences to this melting pot. Early world travellers exchanged and combined food knowledge, and inevitably recipes and our food options have become more complex and interesting, taking influence from contrasting climates, ingredients and cooking methods.

WE'RE HERE TO BRING A WHOLE NEW WORLD OF FLAVOURS TO YOUR DOOR, THROUGH EITHER TRADITIONAL SIERRA LEONEAN OR AFRO-FUSION DISHES.

My own migration story from West Africa to England includes experience gained in Italian kitchens and a culinary school that taught French classics. Settling in Kent, the Garden of England, has afforded me access to many fine ingredients, so this Afro-fusion story continues. In this book, I set out some of my own Afro-fusion recipes, which I hope will prove that diversity can inspire creativity and make for a rich tapestry.

While I was writing *Sweet Salone*, I travelled with photographer Dave Brown to Sierra Leone for the location photography, which was a load of fun. Returning to my great grandmother's village in the Bandajuma Bagbo chiefdom was an emotional experience. The tranquility was lovely and I didn't realise how much I have missed commensality. 'Commensality', the act of eating together, is an important human ritual that has benefits that go beyond the biological need for food, as is well established among food studies scholars. There's something in the process and the sense of community, the shared experience of cooking and eating together, that is really special.

My mission with Shwen Shwen is simple. We're here to bring a whole new world of flavours to your door, through either traditional Sierra Leonean or Afro-fusion dishes. We draw upon our colourful Sierra Leonean culture to bring people closer together through food, offering an authentic experience.

Writing this book taught me a few things: as a chef, not a writer, I prefer to deal with things one at a time and I like process, precision and detail. I like planning and I like flow. I like creativity but see it more as connecting things that in my mind already fit – which is very different to the process of writing a book. I love experimenting; I am naturally curious and yet not particularly good with change or pressure. I don't necessarily enjoy writing. However, I decided to write this book because it's important for me, for Shwen Shwen, and, I hope, for Sierra Leone. This story needs to be told.

I founded Shwen Shwen with a strong sense of purpose and that was to put our Sierra Leonean produce, cuisine and unique culture on the map. I wanted to show that Sierra Leonean cuisine can be fine dining. Ultimately, I wanted to connect people through food; to amplify and elevate our culture where possible. I wanted to prove that creative pursuits can be worthwhile – by creating a platform on which others can build.

I started Shwen Shwen as a way to play my part, using the skills that I have. I am hoping to stimulate a collective pride that we can all share and own. If Shwen Shwen can inspire other Sierra Leoneans, other Africans, other creatives, other women to start something, build something, follow their dreams, then it will have served its purpose. I hope Shwen Shwen can encourage others to become action-takers and impact-makers while pursuing their own dreams.

Maria

A BRIEF HISTORY
OF SIERRA LEONE

ORIGINS

For all time, humanity has sought out great
stories – fictional worlds, dramatic escapes –
in a quest to expand our knowledge of
the world and its origins. Yet, with all
our combined experience and emotional
understanding of the art of storytelling, there
have been no stories greater than those written
by time.

In the present, and for the futures to come,
we find ourselves referring back to these stories.
They are where we find those who represent
us, where we find who we are; and from our
failings, where we find who we want to be. Over
many suns and moons, these stories are baked
into our minds. As every mother recites them to
every child, these stories become suffused into
our blood and take their form as culture.

Instead of a single story, culture is more of
a book or even a collection, with each chapter
having its own voice. Simply put, I hope
to stimulate your senses and open your minds as
each page turns. Using my voice in the best way
I know, I hope to guide you to a small country
on the coast of West Africa. To take you over
proud lion mountains, to show you lambent seas
of cyan and, most importantly, to disclose the
hearts and histories of a nation's people.

I hope to take you to Sierra Leone.

PROLOGUE

At first the land was merely refuge, a passing
salvation. But who could have predicted that
this small expanse, isolated from other African
cultures by dense rainforest and treacherous
mountains, would become the backdrop for
such great stories? How could the Limba
have known that those footsteps were the first
words in the nation's legacy and the dawn of
a new future?

I imagine they would have been apprehensive
as they reached the land. They were leaving
much more than footsteps behind, and they
had little promise of safety in what lay ahead.
But with no other choice, the Limba people
continued and, eventually, after a great deal
of hardship, found a home in the green of the
Wara Wara mountains. It was around the 25th
century BCE that the Limba became the first
inhabitants of Sierra Leone as they escaped
subjugation from the Sahelian kingdoms, a
series of powerful empires in the Sahel region,
the savannah grasslands south of the Sahara.

As news of this land quietly spread, other tribes
seeking refuge from the Sahelian kingdoms'
violence and jihads came to the land, including
the Mende, Loko, Susu, Fula, Temne and
Sherbro. The tribes remained politically
independent but shared a mutual respect for
the land and, despite the several different
languages that were spoken, they observed
similar religious beliefs. Before long, seedlings

began to sprout in rows, pathways were cleared and glowing embers flew at night, forging the foundations of a new human settlement. New trade brought new relationships. The Susu began trading salt, ironwork, gold and clothes (woven by the Fula in the northern savannah) with the coastal and river tribes of the Loko, Limba and Temne.

It was this first gathering and this first accord that marked the birth of the Sierra Leone we know today. The very nature of Sierra Leone's beginning embodies diversity. This willingness to discover and grow was the breakthrough needed to start Sierra Leone's rich food history.

The culture of fusion spawned a cuisine unlike any other. It is said that the Mende people were naturally better at cooking plasas (leafy green sauces), the Krio were skilled in the fine art of fufu (fermented cassava dough balls) and Fula peoples have a distinctive method for cooking granat soup, making it much thicker than other versions. The culture of sharing informed the way food evolved in Sierra Leone, although certain methods and ingredients can be attributed to each tribe. For example, morkor (green banana fritters) were brought to Sierra Leone by the Temne, and although morkor is sold in the country by many vendors not limited to the Temne tribe, it is still recognised as a dish from that culture.

This region of Africa was said to have been first mapped in 1462 by Portuguese explorer Pedro de Sintra, though further investigation suggests it was recorded much earlier by another group of Portuguese explorers in 1446, led by Álvaro Fernandes (there is some debate about exact dates). Upon reaching the land, their sights first fell on a mountain range, with jagged rocks as sharp as claws and greenness that sprung without order, holding the same arrogance as a lion and reflecting its tousled mane. Accordingly, they named the region Sierra Lyoa, which translates as Lion Mountain.

Towards the end of the 15th century, Portuguese ships began visiting more often, enticed by the land of milk and honey that was the Freetown estuary. This estuary is one of the largest natural deep-water harbours in the world and at the time was the greatest harbour on the windward shore. It was a favourite of European mariners, who frequented it to shelter and replenish supplies of fresh water after their long excursions to Africa's shores. It became common for the Portuguese to settle in Serra Lyoa, intermarrying and trading with the local people.

AS EVERY MOTHER RECITES TO
EVERY CHILD, THESE STORIES
BECOME DIFFUSED INTO OUR BLOOD
AND TAKE THEIR FORM AS CULTURE.

Nevertheless, Sierra Leone has a sense of bittersweet: as the moon waxes and wanes and as tides ebb and flow, so our country is riddled with as much tragedy as blessing. This peace could not last for long as the settlers viewed Serra Lyoa only as a solution to their financial and labour problems. Where they could, traders struck deals with the local chiefs to sell the 'undesirables' of their community for European rum, cloth, beads, copper or muskets. Where they couldn't barter, sudden kidnapping raids took place on the coast. The slave trade brought a change to Sierra Leone unlike any other. Slavery came to characterise the land and has destroyed and, regrettably, overshadowed most of the early cultural history of Sierra Leone. The export of the enslaved remained a major business from the late 15th century to the mid-19th century, and it is estimated that at least 74,000 people were being exported annually from West Africa by 1788.

In the midst of this, the Mani (also referred to as Mane or Mande), who lived north of Sierra Leone, began moving south to the eastern coast. From the formulation of their attacks to the intricacy of their defences, the Mani were warriors. Armed with small bows that allowed them to reuse their enemies' arrows but gave no opportunity for the enemy to return the favour, they were unstoppable.

Each warrior had two knives tied to each arm and a shield made of reeds that would have been large enough to cover his entire body. Moving in large groups and growing stronger by turning their captives into soldiers, the Mani routed Sierra Leone, conquering almost all the coastal Indigenous peoples. Their influence is felt today; Sierra Leone's largest ethnic group, the Mende, shows an almost complete convergence of Mani culture. This movement militarised Sierra Leone; the coastal regions had previously been passive but now Mani weapons became a common sight and, consequently, the villages were fortified. Lieutenant R.P.M. Davis' *History of the Sierra Leone Battalion of the Royal West African Frontier Force* (1923) records a British officer who observed one of these fortifications:

'No one who has not seen these fences can realise the immense strength of them. The outer fence at Hahu I measured in several places, and found it to be 2 to 3 feet thick, and most of the logs, or rather trees, of which it was formed, had taken root and were throwing out leaves and shoots.'

Sierra Leone's capital was established in the 18th century by British abolitionists and given its first name: The Province of Freedom. This name is misleading, as I believe the reality of the situation was that the British had found a way to brand themselves as philanthropists, helping to give liberated slaves a better life, while quietly freeing themselves of the burden of having to look after so many refugees.

The result was that few of the people who came to arrive in Sierra Leone had Sierra Leonean heritage. This settlement didn't come off as swimmingly as the British had hoped. Half the settlers died within the first year and the operation failed, miserably. The Province of Freedom was founded on land purchased from local Koya Temne. The Europeans believed they had agreed with the Temne that this land would be the property of the new settlers forever. However, as there were not nearly enough provisions on the land for a permanent settlement, historians have since questioned how much the Temne really understood what they were agreeing to.

In the late 18th century, in 1792, the British seized their second chance by settling 1,196 Nova Scotians (or rather 1,132, as unfortunately 64 of them died on the voyage) in Sierra Leone in the hope things would go better this time.

AS THEY WEARILY CLEARED THE TOWN, THEY UNCOVERED A SOMEWHAT SENTIMENTAL SIGHT. AMID THE THICK FOREST, HIDDEN BEHIND THE UNKEPT FOLIAGE, STOOD A YOUNG COTTON TREE.

The new settlers were mostly liberated American slaves, some of whom had been born in Africa. They had been sent to build a new city on the former 'Granville Town', which was the land that was established by the previous settlers. As they wearily cleared the town, they uncovered a somewhat sentimental sight. Amid the thick forest, hidden behind the unkept foliage, stood a young cotton tree. Today it is the oldest tree in Sierra Leone and stands in perfect emerald majesty, in the middle of a busy crossroads in Sierra Leone's capital. It is said to have been alive since 1787, which suggests that, at the time the settlers came across it, the tree would have been around five years old.

The tree was hailed as a landmark and men, women and children alike gathered round and sang of a new age, a dawning aeon of freedom. On 11 March 1792, a white preacher named Nathaniel Gilbert stood by the tree and gave a sermon; by his side stood Reverend David George who preached the first recorded Baptist service in Africa, and the land was christened 'Freetown'. Even today people pray by the Cotton Tree, making offerings to their ancestors for peace and prosperity.

It may have been out of necessity rather than choice, but Freetown has become the spiritual home of Afro-fusion cooking – a result of the convergence of people from varied backgrounds amid the economic migration of the past few centuries. The city is a place where you could find everyone and everything. The arrival of Muslim traders, followed by Europeans from Portugal, Great Britain and France, the settlement of London's Black Poor, returned slaves from Nova Scotia, Jamaica and other parts of Africa – all have contributed to the city's culture.

So, as this collection we call culture makes its debut and as this book emerges, we find flavours entwined in its pages, ingredients embedded in its sentences and a sense of tradition that courses through its paragraphs. Culture is more than just history. Culture is a state of being that is felt through all of the senses – and at any culture's heart is its food.

STREET FOOD

MAKES ABOUT 20 PIECES

SESAME AND SUNFLOWER SEED SNAPS

This Sierra Leonean street-food snack is sold throughout the country by street vendors. Most of the street vendors are women and children and, for many on the African continent, selling food on the street is the only way to make a living.

This recipe demonstrates the way food cultures have transcended national borders and continents: it originated in Greece and the Middle East more than 6,000 years ago and is popular in East and West Africa, as well as in the African-American community. The African-American celebration of Kwanzaa is based on African harvest festival traditions from various parts of Africa; this snack is a favourite during this time.

sunflower oil, for oiling

100g (3½oz) sesame seeds

50g (1¾oz) sunflower seeds

170g (6oz/¾ cup plus 1½ tbsp) caster (superfine) sugar

85g (3oz) honey

2 tbsp water

Preheat the oven to 180°C/160° fan/350°F/gas mark 4 and very lightly oil a baking sheet and a spatula.

Place both types of seeds on a second baking sheet and toast in the oven for 2–3 minutes until pale golden. Remove and keep warm (the seeds must be warm when added to the sugar mixture).

In a medium saucepan, combine the sugar, honey and water over low heat. As the sugar begins to take on colour, use a fork to encourage the unmelted sugar from the centre to the edge of the pan so it colours evenly. Cook until the mixture reaches 155°C (310°F) when tested on a sugar thermometer. (If you don't have a sugar thermometer, the mixture is ready when it forms a hard piece of toffee that snaps when you drop a spoonful of the mixture into a glass of cool water.)

Once the sugar mixture is ready, you will have to work very quickly. Stir in the warm seed mixture, then tip the mixture onto the oiled baking sheet and spread out into a thin layer using the oiled spatula.

Using a large sharp knife, score the surface at regular intervals so that when it is set you can simply crack along the lines to get nice even shapes. Leave to set for 15–20 minutes.

Store the snaps in an airtight container for up to 1 week. **Note:** You can easily adapt this recipe to make Benne Cakes. Simply omit the sunflower seeds, use 150g (5½oz) sesame seeds and follow the recipe.

GRANAT CAKE

When I was a child, my friends and I would often buy this snack and share a piece between us, crunching it and savouring it as we took the slow meandering walk home from Vine Memorial Secondary School in Freetown, Sierra Leone's capital. I prefer this to Benne Cakes (see Note, opposite) and my top tip is that it can be crushed and sprinkled over vanilla ice cream for added texture and sweetness.

sunflower oil, for oiling

100g (3½oz) unsalted skinless peanuts, finely chopped

150g (1¾oz/¾ cup) caster (superfine) sugar

1 tsp glucose syrup

Preheat the oven to 180°C/160° fan/350°F/gas mark 4 and very lightly oil a baking sheet and a spatula.

Spread out the chopped peanuts on a second baking sheet and toast in the oven for 2–3 minutes. Remove and keep warm (the nuts must be warm when added to the sugar mixture).

In a medium saucepan, combine the sugar and glucose syrup over low heat. As the sugar begins to take on colour, use a fork to encourage the unmelted sugar from the centre to the edge of the pan so it colours evenly. Cook until the mixture reaches 155°C (310°F) when tested on a sugar thermometer. (If you don't have a sugar thermometer, the mixture is ready it forms a hard piece of toffee that snaps when you drop a spoonful of the mixture into a glass of water.)

Once the sugar mixture is ready, you will have to work quickly. Stir in the warm peanuts, tip the mixture onto the oiled baking sheet and spread out using the oiled spatula.

Using a large sharp knife, score the surface at regular intervals so that when it is set you can simply crack along the lines to get nice even shapes.

Store in an airtight container for up to 1 week.

PEPE CHICKEN

This is party food. There are 54 beautiful countries in Africa and one thing they all have in common is African culture. We are party people. Our culture encompasses a love of celebrations that combine food, fashion, music and dance. In my view, no party is complete without pepe chicken. Street vendors in Freetown grill this over hot charcoal throughout the night and it is perfect pre- or post-club. My Salone Fire Chilli Sauce, which is available to buy on my website, is a perfect accompaniment in which fire and flavour dance together (or use chilli sauce of your choice).

10–12 chicken thighs

FOR THE PEPE MARINADE

2 large onions (about 450g/1lb)

20g (¾oz) garlic (about 5 cloves)

25g (1oz) fresh ginger

50ml (2fl oz) lemon juice

1 tbsp curry powder

1 tsp West African Pepper Blend (see opposite)

2 stalks lemongrass

1 tsp sweet paprika

1 tsp ground coriander

2 tsp salt (or to taste)

200g (7oz) unsalted peanut butter (use one without palm oil)

30g (1oz) tomato purée (tomato paste)

130g (4½oz) fresh tomatoes, chopped (about 1 medium tomato)

1 stock cube (use one without MSG) dissolved in 300ml (10½fl oz/1¼ cups plus 1 tbsp) hot water or 300ml (10½fl oz/1¼ cups plus 1 tbsp) chicken, beef, fish or vegetable stock

2–3 scotch bonnet chillies, seeds left in, to taste

For the pepe marinade, put all the ingredients in the bowl of a food processor and blend until smooth and well combined.

Transfer to a saucepan and cook on medium heat for 10–15 minutes, stirring from time to time to prevent sticking, until the marinade has reduced and thickened. Taste and adjust seasoning if needed. Let the marinade cool.

Put the chicken thighs in a large glass or ceramic bowl, pour over half the marinade (you can freeze the rest or keep it for up to 1 week covered in the fridge) and massage it well into the chicken. Cover and set aside to marinate in the fridge for 2–3 hours or overnight.

Preheat the oven to 200°C/180°C fan/400°F/gas mark 6.

Arrange the chicken pieces in a single layer in a baking tin. Roast for 35–40 minutes, basting occasionally, until cooked through (they are ready when the juices run clear when pierced in the thickest part of the thigh with a skewer).

Note: In the warmer months, the thighs can be cooked on the barbecue. Baste them regularly and turn them frequently until they are cooked through, as above.

WEST AFRICAN PEPPER BLEND

This aromatic and spicy blend is at the heart of many of my dishes.

2½ tsp grains of paradise

2 tbsp black peppercorns

2 tbsp white peppercorns

1 tbsp cubeb pepper

3 tbsp allspice berries

Toast all the peppercorns in a dry pan over medium heat until fragrant. Allow to cool then grind in a spice grinder or pestle and mortar. Store in an airtight jar. It will stay fresh for up to 3 months.

PEPE RED SNAPPER COOKED IN BANANA LEAVES

Pepe fish is often prepared using red snapper, which is fished from the warm waters of the Atlantic Ocean, the Caribbean Sea and the Gulf of Mexico. The African red snapper is an exotic fish with a sweet, firm, white, well-textured flesh. Sierra Leone has one of the richest fisheries in West Africa, but fish populations have plummeted since the 1980s because of overfishing, which is having a devastating effect. Without more resources for policing and strong enforcement it will sadly continue. As always, be sure to buy ethically sourced fish from a reliable source.

You can buy fresh or frozen banana leaves from some Asian and Caribbean grocers. If you can't find them, wrap the fish first in baking paper, then in foil.

6 whole snapper (350–450g/12oz–1lb each), cleaned and gutted

salt, for seasoning

300g (10½ oz) Pepe Marinade (see page 22)

banana leaves, for wrapping (optional) or baking paper

lime wedges, to serve

Make 2–3 diagonal slits on the side of each fish. Put the fish in a shallow baking tin, season with salt, spread the Pepe Marinade over the fish and work it well into the slits and the cavity. Cover and leave to marinate in the fridge for 1–2 hours.

Preheat the oven to 200°C/180°C fan/400°F/gas mark 6.

Wrap the fish individually in banana leaves (if you can't get banana leaves, wrap each fish carefully in baking paper). Cook the wrapped fish parcels on a baking sheet for 30–40 minutes depending on the size of the fish. Open one of the parcels and test; if the flesh easily comes away from the bone at the thickest part when tested with a knife, it is cooked. If not, cook for a few minutes longer.

Serve with lime wedges and a green salad on the side, if you like.

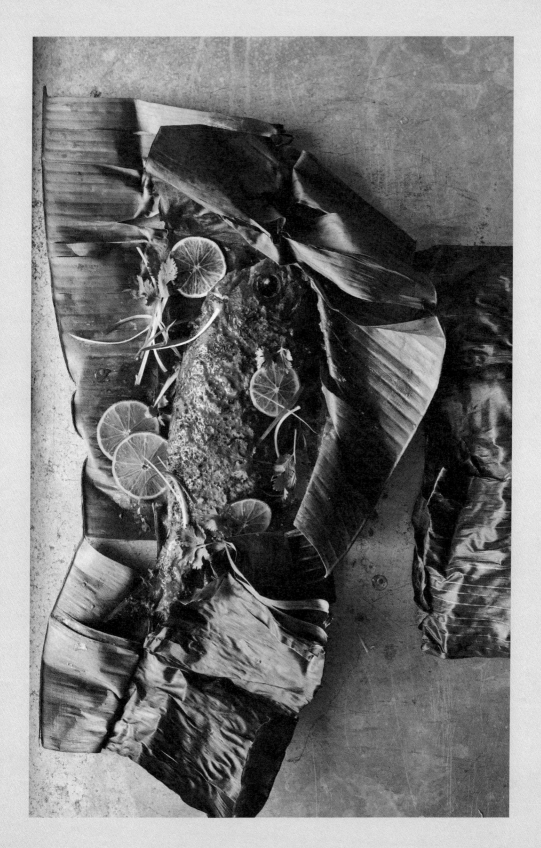

PATCH GRANAT
(TOASTED PEANUTS)

Patch granat is a very popular street food sold in Sierra Leone. It's often sold by women, who carry it around on the street. Empty tomato purée (paste) tins are used to measure. I spoke to Salamatu Kamara, who works for my friend Marianne in Sierra Leone and spent a number of years selling patch granat in Freetown. She told me it sells for Le 5,000 for a 70g (2½oz) tin measurement, which is about 50 pence (80 cents).

In Sierra Leone we enjoy patch granat with freshly baked bread or with garri and sugar for a filling lunch.

The process usually involves sun-drying the peanuts after soaking them in salt water but, as we're a bit sun-deprived in the UK, I've suggested oven-drying the peanuts before toasting.

30g (1oz) pink Himalayan salt

300ml (10½fl oz/1¼ cups plus 1 tbsp) water

150g (5½oz) raw pink-skin peanuts

In a bowl, mix the salt into the measured water until it's fully dissolved. Add the peanuts and leave to soak for 2 hours.

Preheat the oven to 80°C/60°C fan/175°F/lowest gas mark.

After 2 hours, drain the peanuts, spread out in a single layer on a baking sheet and oven-dry for about 1 hour. Leave the oven slightly ajar if you're not using a fan oven to allow moisture from the peanuts to escape.

Increase the heat to 160°C/140°C fan/325°F/gas mark 3 and toast for 25–30 minutes. The peanuts will peel easily and be nicely browned and crunchy when they are ready.

Allow to cool and enjoy with a nice cold beverage.

CHICKEN HUNTU

Chicken huntu – steamed chicken balls in a fonio and seed crust – is a lunchtime street food, often sold at schools. It makes great canapés in that it's a small decorative food that can be held in the fingers and eaten in a single bite. If Africans did hors d'oeuvres or appetizers, then this would be it. I make these frequently at my private-dining events and they're very popular.

FOR THE CHICKEN BALLS

500g (1lb 2oz) chicken breast, chopped

1½ tsp finely chopped fresh ginger

1½ tsp finely chopped garlic

1 medium onion, roughly chopped

1 scotch bonnet chilli, chopped

45g (1½ oz) semolina

2 tbsp olive oil

1 chicken or vegetable stock cube
  (use one without MSG), crumbled

FOR THE FONIO AND SEED CRUST

5½ tbsp toasted sesame seeds

2½ tbsp black sesame seeds

20g (¾oz) fonio

2 tsp caraway seeds

1 tbsp coriander seeds, toasted in
  a dry pan and ground

2 tsp fennel seeds

4 tsp flaxseeds (linseeds)

2 tbsp poppy seeds

2 tsp sweet red pepper flakes

1 tsp sea salt flakes

2 tsp hot chilli flakes, or to taste

1¼ tsp garlic granules

For the chicken balls, put all the ingredients in a food processor and blend until smooth, scraping the sides of the food processor down as you go. Transfer to a bowl, cover and chill in the fridge for 30 minutes.

Meanwhile, prepare a steamer, lining the base with non-stick baking paper.

For the fonio and seed crust, mix all ingredients together in a mixing bowl.

To make the chicken balls, take the chicken mixture out of the fridge. Measure out 1 tablespoon and roll into a ball. Repeat with the remaining mixture. You should have enough for 15–20 chicken balls.

Roll the balls in the fonio and seed mixture to coat well. Put the coated balls in the prepared steamer (trying not cover all the steam holes) and steam for 10–15 minutes or until the balls are cooked through. Cut into one to make sure there is no pink left in the flesh. (You may need to work in batches depending on the size of your steamer.) Serve warm.

FISH HUNTU

Fish huntu is a traditional dish of steamed fish balls commonly sold on the streets of Freetown by Fula women. Fula people are one of the largest ethnic groups in West Africa and are widely dispersed throughout the region. They are predominantly followers of Islam and have traditionally been nomadic, trading and herding cattle, goats and sheep.

I've used haddock, but you could use cod or another white fish such as plaice, coley or pollock. Ensure your fish is responsibly sourced.

FOR THE FISH BALLS

500g (1lb 2oz) haddock fillets, chopped

1½ tsp finely chopped fresh ginger

1½ tsp finely chopped garlic

1 medium onion, roughly chopped

¼ scotch bonnet chilli, chopped

45g (1½ oz) semolina

2 tbsp sunflower oil

1 chicken or vegetable stock cube
(use one without MSG), crumbled

FOR THE SESAME-SEED CRUST

80g (2¾oz) toasted white sesame seeds

15g (½oz) dried ginger flakes

20g (¾oz) black sesame seeds

15g (½oz) dried garlic flakes

4 tsp red pepper flakes

2–3 tsp super-hot chilli flakes (to taste)

TO SERVE

sea salt flakes, to taste

lime wedges

For the fish balls, put all the ingredients in a food processor and blend until smooth, scraping the sides of the food processor down as you go. Transfer to a bowl, cover and chill in the fridge for 30 minutes..

Meanwhile, prepare a steamer, lining the base with non-stick baking paper.

For the sesame-seed crust, mix all ingredients together in a mixing bowl.

To make the fish balls, take the fish mixture out of the fridge. Measure out 1 tablespoon and roll into a ball. Repeat with the remaining mixture. You should have enough for 15–20 fish balls.

Roll the balls in the sesame-seed crust mixture to coat well. Put the coated balls in the prepared steamer and steam for 10–15 minutes. (You may need to work in batches depending on the size of your steamer.) The balls are ready when the flesh is white throughout; cut into one to test.

Serve warm with sea salt flakes and lime wedges.

GARRI KANYAH

Made with groundnuts (peanuts) and garri, dried, toasted, granulated cassava. The dried granules have a texture similar to medium semolina. Note that cassava should not be eaten raw in large quantities because it contains a naturally occurring cyanide that is toxic to humans. Soaking, fermenting and cooking cassava are processes that render the toxin harmless.

Kanyah is a simple snack that's sold all over Sierra Leone. It's naturally gluten free and very simple – just three main ingredients: garri, peanuts and sugar. The women in the villages make kanyah the old-fashioned way – using muscle power to pound it into oblivion. Women in Sierra Leone have muscles of steel and chat away as they work the ingredients to a smooth paste.

360g (12¾oz) ready-made garri (see page 243)

350g (12oz) crunchy peanut butter (use one without palm oil)

50–100g (1¾–3½oz/¼–½ cup) coconut sugar (to taste)

Toast the garri in a dry frying pan until warm and browned.

Put the toasted garri and peanut butter in the bowl of a food processor and blend until smooth (this will take at least 4–5 minutes). Scrape down the sides with a spatula a few times. Taste and add sugar according to your own preference and blend again.

Press the mixture in an even layer in the base of a 20cm (8in) square brownie tin (pan), then cut into squares.

Serve right away or store in an airtight container for up to 4 weeks.

MORKOR WITH SMOKED SALONE FIRE MAYO

Morkor are green banana fritters topped with scotch bonnet aioli. For my version I've used banana and plantain with mayonnaise spiked with smoked paprika and Salone Fire Chilli Sauce. This is a very popular street food in Sierra Leone and a favourite at Shwen Shwen events. Who'd have thought it could become a sought-after party food, perfect for cocktail evenings?

FOR THE FRITTERS

60g (2¼oz/scant ½ cup) plain (all-purpose) flour

5g (1 tsp) baking powder

3 green plantains, finely sliced using a mandoline

3 large ripe bananas, finely sliced

5 spring onions (scallions), finely sliced (white and green parts)

5 tbsp water

sunflower oil, for deep frying

salt and pepper

FOR THE SMOKED SALONE FIRE MAYO

120g (4¼oz) good-quality mayonnaise

1 tbsp smoked paprika

2 tsp Salone Fire Chilli Sauce (or chilli sauce of your choice)

1 tsp lemon juice, or to taste

For the fritters, sift the flour and baking powder together in a large mixing bowl. Add the sliced plantain and banana, spring onion (scallion) and the water. Mix well and season with salt and pepper.

Preheat the oven to 140°C/120°C fan/275°F/gas mark 1.

Heat the oil in a deep, heavy-based pan no more than half full. To test if the oil is hot enough, drop a small amount of the fritter mixture into the hot oil. It should sizzle and rise to the surface right away.

Working in batches, drop tablespoons of the mixture into the hot oil. Fry on both sides until nicely golden, 3–6 minutes in total. Remove with a slotted spoon and drain on a plate lined with paper towels. Keep them warm in the oven and repeat with the remaining mixture. (You should have enough to make about 10–15 fritters.)

For the smoked Salone Fire mayo, put the mayonnaise in a bowl, stir in the paprika and chilli sauce and mix until well combined. Taste and season with lemon juice and salt.

Serve the fritters with the mayo on the side for dipping.

RICE PAP

This is a traditional Sierra Leone recipe, a simple classic that is often served as a starter at social gatherings. If you'd like to make this a little faster, you can dry the balls in the oven at a higher temperature of 110°C/90°C fan/225°F/gas mark ¼ for 2–2½ hours, keeping an eye on them so that they don't colour.

180g (6¼oz/1 cup plus 1 tbsp) rice flour

500ml (17fl oz/2 cups) water

400ml (14fl oz/1¾ cups) coconut milk

50–100g (1¾–3½oz/¼–½ cup) coconut sugar, to taste

TO SERVE

handful toasted coconut chips

mango cubes (optional)

Preheat the oven to 50°C/30°C fan/120°F/lowest gas mark (or as low as your oven will go).

Put the rice flour in a large mixing bowl. Sprinkle the measured water over the rice flour a few tablespoons at a time, rubbing it in with your fingers and shaking the bowl until small dough balls start to form. Continue this process until all the rice flour has come together to form tiny balls, about the size of tapioca balls.

Transfer the dough balls to a baking sheet and dry in the oven for 3–4 hours, until the balls are completely dried. Shake the baking sheet and turn them all occasionally throughout the cooking time to make sure they dry out evenly.

Mix the coconut milk and 300ml (10½fl oz/1¼ cups plus 1 tbsp) water in a large saucepan and bring to the boil. Add the dried dough balls and cook, stirring gently to prevent the balls from clumping together. Continue cooking on medium heat until the mixture has thickened slightly, then add coconut sugar to taste.

Continue to cook, stirring occasionally, for 20–25 minutes or until the mixture has the consistency of loose porridge. Taste and add more sugar if necessary.

Serve hot with toasted coconut chips and mango cubes, if using.

BINCH AKARA

Street vendors sell these fritters on street corners, often with an onion gravy and a bread roll. Children often use their lunch money to buy this snack, and it's also a popular food at funerals and 40-day ceremonies (see page 157).

Soak the beans the night before you want to make this dish; beans that you soak yourself will always have more flavour.

> 350g (12oz) dried black-eyed beans
>
> 350g (1½ large onion), roughly chopped
>
> 1–2 scotch bonnet chillies, seeds left in, roughly chopped (to taste)
>
> vegetable oil or palm oil (or a mixture of both), for deep frying
>
> salt

Put the dried beans in a bowl, pour over water to cover and leave to soak overnight.

The next day, rub the beans in the palms of your hands to remove the skins, continuing until all the skin is removed. Rinse the beans and drain in a sieve (strainer).

Put the peeled beans in a food processor with the onion and chillies and blend until smooth. Transfer to a large mixing bowl and season with salt.

Beat the mixture vigorously using a whisk until the mixture is light and aerated – the idea is to whisk in and trap a bit of air, which will make the fritters lighter. Add a splash of water if the mixture is too thick.

Heat the oil in a deep, heavy-based pan no more than half full. To test if the oil is hot enough, drop a small amount of the fritter mixture into the hot oil. It should sizzle and rise to the surface right away.

Working in batches, drop tablespoons of the mixture into the hot oil. Fry until nicely golden on both sides, about 3–6 minutes in total. Remove with a slotted spoon and drain on a plate lined with paper towels. (You should have enough mixture to make 15–20 fritters.)

Serve hot or cold as a snack.

BREADFRUIT CHIPS

In Sierra Leone, the Mende people call breadfruit *beleful*. The Temne people call it *ma-kant-ma-potho*. Not native to Africa, breadfruit originally came from New Guinea and the Philippines centuries ago and is now commonly found throughout West Africa.

These chips are simple and quick to make. In cooking terms, the white flesh of breadfruit is similar to potato.

½ green breadfruit (100–150g/3½–5½oz), peeled

vegetable oil for deep frying

coarse sea salt

Cut the breadfruit lengthwise into 5mm (¼in) thick slices, then cut into 5mm (¼in) sticks. Try to keep the cuts uniform so the breadfruit cooks evenly.

Soak the breadfruits sticks in cold water for 20 minutes to remove the excess starch and sap. Drain and rinse in three changes of fresh cold water, draining after each rinse. Leave the breadfruit to dry completely in a single layer on a baking sheet lined with a clean dish towel until thoroughly dried – they must be thoroughly dry before they're added to the hot oil.

Heat the oil in a large, deep, heavy-based pan no more than half full. To test if the oil is hot enough, drop a breadcrumb into the hot oil. It should sizzle and turn brown in 20 seconds.

Working in batches, fry the breadfruit sticks in batches, cooking for 2–3 minutes until they are creamier in colour and crispy. Remove with a slotted spoon and drain on a baking sheet lined with paper towels.

Sprinkle generously with salt and serve.

Note: With just a few adjustments to the recipe, you can make cheesy breadfruit chips. Once the chips are cooked, toss with a bit of chilli powder, chipotle powder and garlic powder. Top with grated Cheddar cheese and put in a hot oven until the cheese has melted.

RICE AND BANANA AKARA

Some people have these fritters for breakfast, while others have them for lunch. You can eat them on their own or with stew and bread, as part of a 'fry-fry'. As a street food, they are served on their own, with a sweet onion gravy or in bread as a loaded sandwich.

6 over-ripe bananas or 4 black plantains

85g (3oz/½ cup) rice flour

2 tsp freshly grated nutmeg

2 tsp baking powder

sunflower oil, for deep-frying

Blend the bananas or plantains in a blender or food processor until smooth. Transfer to a large bowl and add the rice flour, nutmeg and baking powder.

Mix well and leave rest for 30 minutes.

Heat the oil in a deep, heavy-based pan no more than half full. To test if the oil is hot enough, drop a small amount of the fritter mixture into the hot oil. It should sizzle and rise to the surface right away.

Working in batches, drop tablespoons of the mixture into the hot oil. Fry on both sides until nicely golden, 3–6 minutes in total. Remove with a slotted spoon and drain on a plate lined with paper towels. (You should have enough to make about 15–20 fritters.)

Serve hot or cold as a snack.

SHWEN SHWEN DOUGHNUTS

The origin of the doughnut is a matter of some dispute. One theory is that these fried dough balls were invented by the British and the earliest English-language record of a doughnut recipe dates back to the wife of a doctor in Hertford, England in 1800. Baroness Elizabeth Dimsdale's recipe for 'dow nuts' were taken from a local cook, known only as Mrs Fordham. She also used nutmeg and deep-fried them in hog's lard. Given that Sierra Leone was a British colony from 1808 it is reasonable to assume that Sierra Leoneans inherited this recipe from the British.

Unlike traditional doughnuts made with yeast, these are made using baking powder as a raising agent, which makes the process quicker. At Shwen Shwen private dining events, we serve these for dessert with a butterscotch sauce and vanilla ice cream.

300g (10½oz/2¼ cups) plain (all-purpose) flour, sifted

2 tsp baking powder

100g (3½oz/½ cup) coconut sugar

½ tsp salt

1 tsp freshly grated nutmeg

3 large eggs, beaten

2 tsp vanilla extract

120ml (4¼fl oz/½ cup) milk

120g (4¼oz/9 tbsp) butter, melted

sunflower oil for deep frying

Combine the flour, baking powder, coconut sugar, salt and nutmeg in a large mixing bowl.

Make a well in the middle and stir in the eggs, vanilla extract, milk and melted butter. Mix thoroughly until all the ingredients are well combined and the batter is smooth and lump-free.

Heat the oil in a wok or a large, deep, heavy-based pan or wok no more than half full. To test if the oil is hot enough, drop a bit of the batter into the hot oil. It should sizzle and turn brown in 20 seconds.

Using two spoons (one to scoop and the other to scrape), drop spoonfuls of the batter into the hot oil. Fry in small batches, making sure pan is not over-crowded. You should have enough batter to make about 15–50 doughnuts.

Fry the doughnuts until they are nice and golden, turning once or twice. Remove with a slotted spoon and drain on a baking sheet lined with paper towels.

Serve warm or cold.

AFRO-FUSION STARTƐRS

THE BEGINNING

It is a task that is easier said than done: to mark the explicit beginning or to predict the definite end to one's story. After much consideration, I believe my story began with my great-grandmother, Madame Isata Kamara. She was born in Kánkàn, Guinea, which neighbours Sierra Leone, and lived a humble life as the youngest of three siblings. Her family worked in the kola nut trade, for which Kánkàn was especially well known during the late 19th century, and the family members frequently travelled back and forth between Sierra Leone and Guinea trading kola nuts for gold.

Through the eyes of a stranger, as my great-grandmother was, Sierra Leone would have been intimidating. There would have been lots going on, in positive and maybe negative ways. My great-grandmother would have met many different types of people – some quite friendly, perhaps some who were overly so, in an overbearing kind of way. A stranger would hear people conversing in two completely different languages yet somehow still understanding each other with perfect fluency. There would be different smells, some sweet some not quite so, and different sights encompassing the extravagant through to the humble. To a stranger, Sierra Leone would have been exciting.

But this feeling was not to last. One day, Isata's father travelled back to Guinea for more stock and on his way came to an untimely death. To make matters worse, due to an unfortunate set of circumstances, Isata's family was left stranded in Sierra Leone. From that point on, Isata's life would not be easy. You'll learn through reading my story that Sierra Leonean women – above all else – are resilient.

As she grew older, Isata became known as Mama Iye. She was a farmer, revered by her community and known to be a kind, generous and peaceful person. Because of her kind temperament, many people that met her named their children after her.

She married a son from the Kabba family in Majihun, a village very close to Senbehun in the Southern Province of Sierra Leone, and had three children. After the death of her husband, she returned to her mother's lands in Bandajuma in the Southern Province of Sierra Leone and, after many years, she remarried.

When Mama Iye met her second husband, Maada Brima, the only family known to visit him was his sister. He had no children and the couple would not have any children of their own. Maada Brima Fambuleh was from the Pujehun District and was of Liberian descent. He wished for nothing more than his beloved wife. Mama Iye was the breadwinner of the family, and Maada Brima cherished her. Relatives have told me he was a very strict and proud man but that the couple never argued. What Mama Iye said was final. His usual prayer was that he would die before her, for if

MY GRANDMOTHER WAS SOMETHING OF A MAGICIAN WHEN IT CAME TO HER SOURCING AND USE OF INGREDIENTS; ABSOLUTELY NOTHING WOULD BE WASTED AND EFFICIENCY WAS HER FORTE.

she were to leave him first his suffering would be unbearable. Maada Brima's prayers were answered, for he died long before Mama Iye and long before the rebel war in Sierra Leone, which began in 1991.

Mama Iye's youngest child was Mariama Kabba – my grandmother, who is still alive to this day, although no one knows how old she truly is. At that time, it wasn't the done thing to make a fuss of one's birthday. She remembers an earthquake from 1945 in great detail, so we assume she is in her nineties. My great-grandfather, Pa Fodie Kabba, asked his daughter Mariama to marry his friend's son, named Gaamoh Abdullah Bawoh. With him she also had three children: Fatmata (my mother), Isatu and Fomba (who unfortunately died aged 26 in an accident).

Sadly, this was not a blissful marriage. In the words of my mother, 'E nor bin dae take good care of am en e bin dae beat am'. Sierra Leone has a long, bleak history of sexual and gender-based violence. Its cruel patriarchal attitudes were present then and have not faded even now. Although the cases and rates of violence in developing countries like Sierra Leone are more extreme, I must stress that this is a worldwide issue.

Many of you reading this as of now will have heard a similar story from someone close, or maybe even have lived through it. Forgive my slight tangent here, but I believe it is important

to say that, as a society, we must do better at holding men accountable, at teaching our sons right from wrong and making sure the voices of women are heard. This isn't only about saving those who are subject to gender and sexual-based violence (crucial on its own), but about creating a future in which we protect the vulnerable. I'm exceedingly proud of my grandmother for leaving her husband, especially in a generation that frowned upon the idea. To this day she is my greatest idol, and it would be an honour to inherit even an ounce of her strength of character.

Where there is tradition, there is my grandmother; she is the embodiment of it – although this presents itself in good and bad ways. To give you a picture of her, I'd say she's horridly stuck in her ways, yet curiously endearing in her manner. Even in her old age she insists on living a rural life outside the Southern Province city of Bo, continuing her family's kola nut trade, and surrounded by all that is familiar.

Looking back, those childhood memories are some of my most treasured. Perhaps this is a universal experience, but there are certain times when, as a child, you realise that your parents were also children, and that they are not as steadfast, as mature as they wish you to believe. To me, this became apparent when my grandmother visited when I was a child in Freetown.

Everyone considered my mother to be a great cook. A simple stew made just to use up a few ingredients was enough to call the entire neighbourhood by its aroma, and dinner times were never lonely. Yet my grandmother could find fault in everything my mother did, from her choice of ingredients to simply the way she would cut a single onion. I won't evaluate who was the better cook for fear of stirring a hornet's nest – although my grandmother was a talent in the kitchen.

As much as my grandmother has inspired me in life, her teachings are what move me in the kitchen. I would not be the chef and the person I am today without her. An old mantra that always drew an arctic chill through my childhood home on the equator was: 'You waste too much,' or that, 'There was no need for this amount fish,' or 'Why would you throw this out? No! You have to use up!'

She wasn't just nagging when she made these comments. My grandmother was something of a magician; absolutely nothing would be wasted, and efficiency was her forte. She would slice onions, put them in a jar and top the jar off with water. This preserves the onions, keeping them fragrant and sharp so she didn't have to use many to make the dish flavourful, and the water could also be used in cooking. Another trick would be to fry (or dry) fish and cover it with palm oil to provide an airtight seal, extending its shelf life.

It was through her I learned the value of quality produce. Living in the UK, which wastes 9.5 million tonnes of food per year, I make it my mission to follow in my grandmothers footsteps, ensuring nothing that can be used ever goes to waste in my kitchen.

GOOSE FAT OVEN-BAKED PLANTAIN CHIPS WITH ROAST GARLIC MAYO

If you're craving something salty and crunchy, here it is. Plantain chips are naturally gluten free and paleo-friendly.

Plantains are a member of the banana family, but they are starchy, not sweet. These fruits can be green, yellow or almost black, according to how ripe they are. Plantain is a staple food in Sierra Leone and West Africa, where they are mostly grown in small-scale compound gardens, and West Africa is one of the main plantain-producing regions of the world.

When plantains are green and unripe, they have a chalky texture and flavour resembling a potato. It's worth mentioning that plantains should not be eaten raw; they're not harmful but the flesh is bitter and unpleasant. Once cooked, boiled, fried, baked or roasted, however, they have a wonderful flavour.

FOR THE ROASTED GARLIC MAYO

6 garlic cloves, unpeeled

120g (4¼oz) good-quality mayonnaise

1 tsp lemon juice, or to taste

salt

FOR THE PLANTAIN CHIPS

2 yellow plantains

2 tbsp goose fat

1 tsp garlic salt

1 tsp cayenne pepper

1 tsp sweet paprika

sea salt flakes

Preheat the oven to 200°C/180°C fan/400°F/gas mark 6.

Begin with the roast garlic mayo. Wrap the garlic cloves in foil and roast until the flesh is soft, about 30 minutes (you can roast the plantain chips at the same time, see below). Allow to cool, then remove the garlic flesh using a teaspoon (discard the skins). Mash the flesh and mix it into the mayonnaise, stir in the lemon juice and season with salt.

If you're not using the mayo right away, cover and chill in the fridge until needed.

For the plantain chips, top and tail the plantains. Use a sharp knife to cut a vertical slit through the skins, then peel away and discard the skins. Slice into even chip-sized pieces and put in a bowl.

Add the goose fat, garlic salt, cayenne pepper and paprika to the chips and mix well. Spread the chips in a single layer on a baking sheet and bake in the hot oven for 25–30 minutes, turning once.

Sprinkle with sea salt flakes and serve warm with the roasted garlic mayo on the side.

CASSAVA AND PARMESAN CROQUETTES WITH ROAST GARLIC MAYO AND PARMESAN SHAVINGS

These croquettes work as an appetizer, snack or as part of a main course. They are a tasty finger food, or, if made larger, can be served as a first course. This dish is a favourite at my supper-club events.

Cassava is an important source of dietary carbohydrates in the tropical and subtropical areas of the world. The tuberous roots, with their hard, starchy white flesh, provide food for more than 500 million people. Note that cassava should not be eaten raw in large quantities because it contains a naturally occurring cyanide that is toxic to humans. Soaking, fermenting and cooking cassava are processes that render the toxin harmless.

FOR THE CROQUETTES

1kg (2lb 4oz) cassava, peeled and chopped

1 tsp salt, plus extra to season

3 tbsp butter

4 tbsp double (heavy) cream

2 large eggs, lightly beaten

1 tsp freshly grated nutmeg

3 tbsp chopped parsley

250g (9oz) Parmesan, grated

1 tsp ground white pepper

oil for deep frying

FOR THE COATING

100g (3½oz/¾ cup) plain (all-purpose) flour seasoned with salt and white pepper

3 eggs, beaten

200g (7oz) panko breadcrumbs

TO SERVE

Roast Garlic Mayo (see page 50)

Parmesan shavings

For the croquettes, put the cassava in a large pan, fill with cold water, add the 1 tsp salt and bring to the boil over high heat. Reduce the heat to medium and cook until the cassava is tender all the way through when tested with a fork. Drain and transfer to a large bowl. Add the butter and cream and mash using a potato masher until smooth.

Once the mixture is smooth, add the 2 beaten eggs, nutmeg, parsley and grated Parmesan. Mix thoroughly and season to taste with salt and white pepper.

For the coating, prepare 3 bowls: one for seasoned flour, a second for the 3 beaten eggs and a third for the panko breadcrumbs.

One large tablespoon at a time, shape the cassava mixture into neat cylinder-shaped croquettes. Place them on a large plate and continue until all the cassava mixture is shaped into croquettes.

Roll each croquette first in the flour, then dip into the beaten egg and finally roll in the breadcrumbs, making sure they are thoroughly covered. You should have enough for 10–15 croquettes. Place the coated croquettes on a plate and refrigerate for 1 hour.

Heat the oil in a wok or a large, deep, heavy-based pan no more than half full. To test if the oil is hot enough, drop a breadcrumb into the hot oil. It should sizzle and turn brown in 20 seconds.

Working in batches, fry the croquettes in the hot oil for 3–5 minutes or until golden brown and cooked through. Remove using a slotted spoon and drain on a baking sheet lined with paper towels.

Serve warm, sprinkled with the Parmesan shavings, with the Roast Garlic Mayo on the side.

CURED AND BLOW-TORCHED MACKEREL WITH HIBISCUS AND GINGER SAUCE

Up and down Sierra Leone's 400-km (250-mile) Atlantic Ocean coastline, fishermen go to sea every day to feed their families. Mackerel can be caught anywhere from Norway to South Africa. It is a rich fish and the tartness of the hibiscus cuts straight through, complementing the smoky, oily flesh beautifully.

When I was growing up in Freetown, my mum never liked mackerel (we get the type known as horse mackerel in Sierra Leone). She considered it a cheap, oily fish that doesn't taste nice and smells funny. I always liked it because it has fewer bones and is meaty. Paired with hibiscus and ginger, it makes a perfect spring supper, and I love the charred taste from the mackerel skin. This is a delicate dish with depths of flavour.

Soak the hibiscus for the sauce the day before you plan to eat this dish.

FOR THE HIBISCUS AND GINGER SAUCE

30g (1oz) dried hibiscus flowers

650ml (22fl oz/2¾ cups) water

30g (1oz/2½ tbsp) granulated sugar, or to taste

1–2 tsp freshly grated ginger, to taste

10g (¼oz/2 tsp) butter

FOR THE CURED MACKEREL

4 mackerel fillets, pin bones removed (ask your fish supplier to do this for you)

100g (3½oz) fine sea salt

100g (3½oz) caster (superfine) sugar

1 tbsp fennel seeds, toasted and ground in a pestle and mortar or spice grinder

1 tbsp coriander seeds, toasted and ground in a pestle and mortar or spice grinder

1 tbsp West African Pepper Blend (see page 23)

fresh dill sprigs, to serve

For the hibiscus and ginger sauce, put the hibiscus flowers in a small pan, pour over the measured water and leave overnight to rehydrate. The next day, bring the soaked hibiscus flowers to a boil, turn down the heat and simmer for 40 minutes. Transfer to a food processor or blender, whizz until smooth, then pass through a fine sieve (strainer) into a clean pan. Add the sugar and cook over a high heat until the sauce has reduced to a syrupy consistency, 10–15 minutes. Add grated ginger until you can really taste it coming through and beat in the butter, which should melt in the residual heat of the sauce.

Taste and add more sugar if you think it needs it; the sauce should have a sharpness to it as a foil to the richness of the mackerel. Set aside and keep warm.

For the cured mackerel, mix the salt, sugar and spices together. Lay the mackerel fillets flat in the base of a glass or ceramic dish. Sprinkle the curing mixture over the mackerel to cover evenly and leave to cure for about 12 minutes. (**Note:** The mackerel can be cured for up to 1 hour if you prefer a more 'cured' taste and texture; see page 120.)

Rinse the mackerel fillets under cold water to remove the curing mixture. Pat dry with paper towels, and, using a kitchen blowtorch, scorch the skin of the mackerel on both sides until charred and the fish is cooked through, 2–3 minutes in total. (Hold the blowtorch a few inches from the fish and gently move around, not scorching any one bit for too long.)

Alternatively, heat the grill to high and grill for 3–4 minutes (be careful not to burn them). Serve the fillets with the warm hibiscus and ginger sauce, garnished with dill.

KANKANKAN SPICE MIX

In Sierra Leone, this traditional peanut-based street food spice has been tantalizing tastebuds for decades, and it's often used to marinate meat. The most popular area for kankankan is in Freetown, outside the Youyi Building, Brookfields, where several government ministry offices are located.

I have read that this spice originated from Niger and Mali from the Hausa people. Some say it comes from northern Nigeria. I have also been told it is widely used in Burkina Faso and I know in Cameroon it's called kankan rather than kankankan. Additionally, the fact that there is a city in Guinea that was founded by the Soninke people in the 18th century and became an important trading centre for kola nuts and other goods has got to be another plausible option. Any African historians are welcome to get in touch and provide some answers!

6 strands grains of selim

3 calabash nutmeg

1 whole alligator pepper (grind both the pod and seeds)
or 1 tbsp ground black cardamom

1 tbsp smoked scotch bonnet chilli flakes or powder

100g (3½oz) Spiced Peanuts (see page 60), chopped

2½ tbsp ground ginger

2 tbsp garlic powder

2 tbsp onion powder

3 tbsp smoked paprika

1 tsp salt

Using a coffee grinder, grind the grains of selim, calabash nutmeg, alligator pepper or black cardamom and scotch bonnet chilli flakes to a powder and add to a frying pan.

Add the peanuts and the rest of the spices to the coffee grinder and grind again briefly; avoid over-processing. Add to the frying pan along with the salt. Stir everything together well.

Heat the pan over medium heat and, using a wooden spoon, toss the spice mixture in the pan for about 5 minutes or until you can smell the aroma. Be careful not to let the spices burn.

Turn off heat, set aside and leave to cool. Store the kankankan spice mixture in a sealed jar in a cool dry place for up to 2 months.

KANKANKAN CHICKEN LOLLIPOPS

Chicken lollipops are essentially French-trimmed chicken drumsticks, which means the bones are scraped clean of meat with a sharp knife prior to cooking. The presentation of this dish is elegant, and it makes a great no-mess appetizer course. They're always a hit and parties are not the same without them.

If you prefer, you can ask your butcher to French trim the drumsticks for you, in which case you can skip step 2 of the method below.

12 whole skin-on chicken drumsticks

300g (10½oz) natural yoghurt

5 tbsp Kankankan Spice Mix (see opposite)

1 chicken stock cube (use one without MSG), crumbled

For the drumsticks, using a sharp boning knife chop through the top of the chicken drumsticks at the joint to remove the knuckle.

Turn the drumsticks upside-down and chop the bottom of the bone off using a sharp knife. (This is for aesthetics and not essential.) Push the meat down towards the bottom of the bone so that it looks like a little ball at the bottom of the drumstick. Using tweezers, pull the tendons from the bone and discard. Set the drumsticks aside.

In a large bowl, combine the yoghurt and Kankankan Spice Mix and mix until well combined.

Sprinkle the stock cube over the drumsticks, add the drumsticks to the yoghurt marinade and mix until well coated. Cover with cling film (plastic wrap) and chill in fridge for at least 4 hours or overnight.

When the drumsticks have marinated, preheat the oven to 200°C/180°C fan/400°F/gas mark 6.

Remove the drumsticks from the marinade, shaking off any excess. Sit the drumsticks upright on their bases on a baking tin, then roast for 15–20 minutes or until the marinade has browned and the chicken is cooked through (they are cooked when the juices run clear when tested with a skewer at the thickest part and no trace of pink meat remains).

Serve warm as a canapé or as a starter or appetizer with a side salad.

KANKANKAN CAULIFLOWER FRITTERS WITH YOGHURT AND MAYO SAUCE

Cauliflower fritters pair perfectly with a cool dollop of yogurt and mayo sauce. Cauliflower is part of the *Brassica oleracea* species, which includes other common vegetables such as kale, broccoli and brussels sprouts. Believe it or not, all of these vegetables stem from the cultivation of one single plant: the wild cabbage. If you want a low-carb alternative to, say, potatoes, then cauliflower is for you. Plus, an average serving has a higher quantity of Vitamin C than an orange.

FOR THE CAULIFLOWER FRITTERS

2 medium cauliflower, cut into bitesize florets

sunflower oil for deep frying

260g (9¼oz) gram (chickpea) flour

3 tbsp Kankankan Spice Mix (see page 56)

1 tsp baking powder

330–350ml (11–12fl oz) soda water (club soda)

FOR THE YOGHURT AND MAYO SAUCE

5 tbsp good-quality mayonnaise

5 tbsp Greek yoghurt

5 tsp Kankankan Spice Mix

salt and pepper

Put the cauliflower florets in a heatproof bowl and pour over boiling water to cover. Let the florets sit for 10 minutes then drain, pat dry and set aside.

Meanwhile, make the yoghurt and mayo sauce. Put the mayonnaise, yoghurt and Kankankan Spice Mix in a bowl. Mix thoroughly, taste and season.

Heat the oil in a wok or a large, deep heavy-based pan no more than half full.

While the oil is heating, whisk in a bowl the gram (chickpea) flour, Kankankan Spice Mix and baking powder. Whisk in the soda water (club soda) a little at a time to form a batter with the consistency of pancake batter (you may not need to use it all).

To test if the oil is hot enough, drop some of the batter into the hot oil. It should sizzle and turn brown in 20 seconds.

Working in batches, fry the fritters in the hot oil for 8–10 minutes until golden brown and cooked through. Remove using a slotted spoon, drain on a baking sheet lined with paper towels and keep warm.

Serve with the yoghurt and mayo sauce.

SPICED PEANUTS

Spicy, salty peanuts are a great snack to nibble on between meals or with a few drinks while chatting with friends.

In many parts of Africa, peanuts are known as groundnuts because the nut pods grow underground. They're not actually nuts, but a member of the legume family (as are soybeans and lentils). Peanuts play an important nutritional role in many parts of Africa because they are high in fats and protein, both of which are important in helping to combat child malnutrition. They grow well in semi-arid regions and are a staple food as well as a revenue source for farmers.

1 tsp ground allspice

1 tsp freshly grated nutmeg

1 tsp ground coriander

1 tsp ground ginger

1 tsp cinnamon

¼ tsp chilli powder

1 tsp salt

1 tbsp peanut oil

400g (14oz) unsalted skinless peanuts

Preheat the oven to 170°C/150°C fan/325°F/gas mark 3.

Mix all the spices in a bowl with the oil, then stir in the peanuts and mix until the nuts are well coated.

Spread the nuts in a single layer over a baking sheet and bake for 20–25 minutes, keeping a close eye on the peanuts to ensure they don't burn. Allow to cool completely before serving.

Stored in clean jar, the nuts will keep for up to 2 months.

FISH HUNTU WITH LEMONGRASS SOUP

This is my Afro-fusion version of the traditional dish of steamed fish balls commonly sold on the streets of Freetown by Fula women (see page 32). I've used haddock, but you could use cod or another white fish such as plaice, coley or pollock. As ever, ensure your fish is responsibly sourced.

Lemongrass is a multipurpose herb, used in culinary and medicinal applications. and is widely known for its rich citrus scent. The lemongrass plant itself is not consumed directly, but is used to add flavour to dishes. For this soup, make sure that you peel off the outside leaves and bash the stalk a little for maximum flavour.

Grains of paradise are seeds from the *Aframonum melegueta* plant. They are an aromatic spice that look like peppercorns but with their origin firmly in West Africa and with notes of cardamom, coriander, citrus, ginger, nutmeg and juniper. They pack a light peppery heat, making them a great spice for seasoning, and are also known as melegueta pepper, guinea grains and guinea pepper (grains of selim are also sometimes known as guinea pepper). It should not be confused with alligator pepper.

FOR THE LEMONGRASS AND GINGER SOUP

2 litres (70fl oz/8¾ cups) fish stock

6 stalks lemongrass, bashed

40g (1½oz) garlic, peeled and bashed (about 10 cloves)

50g (1¾oz) fresh ginger, peeled and bashed

20 grains of paradise

½ tsp salt

30g (1oz) fresh coriander, chopped, to garnish (optional)

FOR THE FISH BALLS

500g (1lb 2oz) haddock fillets, chopped

1½ tsp finely chopped fresh ginger

1½ tsp finely chopped garlic

1 medium onion, roughly chopped

¼ scotch bonnet chilli, chopped

45g (1½ oz) semolina

2 tbsp sunflower oil

1 chicken or vegetable stock cube (use one without MSG), crumbled

FOR THE SESAME-SEED CRUST

80g (2¾oz) toasted white sesame seeds

15g (½oz) dried ginger flakes

20g (¾oz) black sesame seeds

15g (½oz) dried garlic flakes

4 tsp red pepper flakes

2–3 tsp super-hot chilli flakes (to taste)

For the lemongrass and ginger soup, put all the ingredients in a large saucepan. Bring to the boil, reduce the heat and simmer for 40 minutes. Turn off the heat and leave to cool.

Strain the soup and pass it through a piece of muslin (cheesecloth). Discard the aromatic flavourings. Taste and adjust the seasoning of the soup then set aside and keep warm.

For the fish balls, put all the ingredients in a food processor and blend until smooth, scraping the sides of the food processor down as you go. Transfer to a bowl, cover and chill in the fridge for 30 minutes.

For the sesame-seed crust, mix all ingredients together in a mixing bowl.

Prepare a steamer, lining the base with non-stick baking paper (try not to cover all the steam holes).

To make the fish balls, take the fish mixture out of the fridge. Measure out 1 tablespoon and roll into a ball. Repeat with the remaining mixture. You should have enough for 10–20 fish balls.

Roll the balls in the sesame-seed crust mixture to coat well. Put the coated balls in the prepared steamer and steam for 10 minutes. (You may need to work in batches depending on the size of your steamer.) The balls are ready when the flesh is white throughout; cut into one to test.

Serve the fish balls with the warm lemongrass and ginger soup and garnish with the coriander if you wish.

CHICKEN HUNTU WITH FONIO AND SEED CRUST AND LEMONGRASS SOUP

Lemongrass *(Cymbopogon citratus)* is grown in Koinadugu, Yele and Kono Districts in Sierra Leone. Native to India and Africa, it is widely used in Thai and Vietnamese cooking, too. Lemongrass is a perennial, so once you plant it, the grass comes back year after year. This is an adaptation of the Sierra Leonean street food huntu (see page 32), using another African ingredient, lemongrass, and the result is lighter. This dish reminds me of rainy season in Sierra Leone.

Cultivated in West Africa, fonio is an ancient African grain. Fonio is drought-tolerant, grown year-round and is considered to be a sustainable, nutritious, gluten-free food.

FOR THE LEMONGRASS AND GINGER SOUP

2 litres (70fl oz/8¾ cups) strong fish stock

6 stalks lemongrass, bashed

40g (1½oz) garlic, peeled and bashed (about 10 cloves)

50g (1¾oz) fresh ginger, peeled and bashed

10 black peppercorns

½ tsp salt

FOR THE CHICKEN BALLS

500g (1lb 2oz) chicken breast, chopped

1½ tsp finely chopped fresh ginger

1½ tsp finely chopped garlic

1 medium onion, roughly chopped

1 scotch bonnet chilli, chopped

45g (1½ oz) semolina

2 tbsp olive oil

1 chicken or vegetable stock cube (use one without MSG), crumbled

FOR THE FONIO AND SEED CRUST

5½ tbsp toasted sesame seeds

2½ tbsp black sesame seeds

20g (¾oz) fonio

2 tsp caraway seeds

1 tbsp coriander seeds, toasted in a dry pan and ground

2 tsp fennel seeds

4 tsp flaxseeds (linseeds)

2 tbsp poppy seeds

2 tsp sweet red pepper flakes

1 tsp sea salt flakes

2 tsp hot chilli flakes, or to taste

1¼ tsp garlic granules

For the lemongrass and ginger soup, put all the ingredients in a large saucepan. Bring to the boil, reduce the heat and simmer for 40 minutes. Turn off heat and leave to cool.

Strain the soup and pass it through a piece of muslin (cheesecloth). Discard the aromatic flavourings. Taste and adjust the seasoning of the soup then set aside and keep warm.

For the chicken balls, put all the ingredients in a food processor and blend until smooth, scraping the sides of the food processor down as you go. Transfer to a bowl, cover and chill in the fridge for 30 minutes.

Meanwhile, prepare a steamer, lining the base with non-stick baking paper.

For the fonio and seed crust, mix all ingredients together in a mixing bowl.

To make the chicken balls, take the chicken mixture out of the fridge. Measure out 1 tablespoon and roll into a ball. Repeat with the remaining mixture. You should have enough for 15–20 chicken balls.

Roll the balls in the fonio and seed mixture to coat well. Put the coated balls in the prepared steamer (trying not cover all the steam holes) and steam for 10–15 minutes or until the balls are cooked through. Cut into one to make sure there is no pink left in the flesh. (You may need to work in batches depending on the size of your steamer.)

Serve warm with the warm lemongrass and ginger soup.

EGUSI, SWEET POTATO AND GOAT'S CHEESE BREAD

Despite enduring many hardships, including civil war, I have lots of fond memories of my childhood in Freetown, one of which has given me a lifelong love of fresh bread. My mum used to buy fresh bread every morning from the local baker, Kortor Barry (*kortor* means 'brother' in Fulani language).

For me, the return to home-baking was one of the few pleasant surprises of the Covid-19 lockdowns, when baking bread was one of my most comforting pastimes.

200g (7oz/1½ cups) strong white bread flour, plus extra to dust

75g (2⅔ oz/½ cup plus ½ tbsp) strong wholemeal (wholewheat) bread flour

7g (2¼ tsp) fast-action dried yeast

5g (¾ tsp) salt

100g (3½oz) sweet potato, finely grated

2 tsp balsamic vinegar

130ml (4fl oz/½ cup) warm water

80g (2¾oz) egusi seeds, plus extra for topping

60g (2¼oz) mild goat's cheese, crumbled

oil, for greasing

1 large egg, beaten and sieved

butter, to serve

Put both types of flour, the yeast, salt, grated sweet potato, balsamic vinegar and water into a large bowl and mix briefly to combine. Cover and leave for 30 minutes.

Add the egusi seeds and goat's cheese and knead for about 10 minutes until the dough is smooth and elastic.

Put the dough in an oiled bowl, cover with oiled cling film (plastic wrap) and allow to rise until doubled in volume, about 1 hour.

With floured hands, divide the dough into 6 equal parts and shape into balls. Take one ball and gently stretch and pull the dough towards the top, creating a smooth surface underneath. Turn the dough over so the smooth side is uppermost and neaten the roll with your hands. Shape the other rolls in the same way, working quickly to ensure the first ones do not over-prove.

Place the rolls on a lightly greased baking sheet, leaving space between them for them to spread as they bake. Lightly pat down the tops to flatten them a little.

Cover loosely with cling film and allow to prove (rise for a second time) in a warm place until one and a half times their original volume. Meanwhile, preheat the oven to 200°C/180°C fan/400°F/gas mark 6.

Brush the top of each roll with the beaten egg and sprinkle with the extra egusi.

Bake for about 15 minutes, or until nicely golden. Serve warm with whipped butter.

TIGER PRAWNS WITH SALONE FIRE CHILLI BUTTER AND BURNT LEMON

Tiger prawns (jumbo shrimp) are like the tomahawk steak of the sea. Prawns are caught widely off the coast of West Africa, and they have a buttery texture and firmness that makes them ideal for flash frying. When their flavour is mixed with burnt lemon and Salone Fire chilli butter, it's a taste sensation. As ever, be sure to buy seafood from a reliable and sustainable source.

FOR THE SALONE FIRE CHILLI BUTTER

1 tbsp olive oil

1 large plum tomato, peeled, deseeded and chopped

1–2 tsp Salone Fire Chilli Sauce (or chilli sauce of your choice)

large pinch of caster (superfine) sugar

110g (3¾oz/7¾ tbsp) unsalted butter, at room temperature

zest of 1 lime

2 tbsp finely chopped coriander (cilantro)

salt and pepper

FOR THE BURNT LEMON

1–2 tsp icing (confectioners') sugar

2 unwaxed lemons, halved

FOR THE PRAWNS

sunflower oil, for greasing

12 large tiger prawns (jumbo shrimp), preferably with the shells on

For the Salone Fire chilli butter, heat the olive oil in a pan, add the tomato and cook, stirring, for 3–4 minutes. Add the Salone Fire Chilli Sauce and sugar and season with salt. Continue to cook, stirring, until the mixture is thick and reduced, 15–20 minutes.

Remove from the heat, allow to cool, then mash in the butter to make a smooth paste. Mix in the lime zest and coriander (cilantro). Taste and adjust the seasoning.

For the burnt lemons, heat a frying pan over a medium heat. Put the icing (confectioners') sugar on a small plate, then dip the lemon halves into it and coat well. When the pan is hot, add the lemon halves, cut-side down, and cook without turning until the lemons are dark and caramelized. Set aside.

For the prawns (shrimp), lightly oil the prawns and season with salt and pepper. Heat a frying pan until hot, then add the prawns and sear, turning once, until they are pink. Reduce the heat and add half of the Salone Fire chilli butter to the pan. Allow to melt and baste the prawns with the butter for 2–3 minutes or until cooked through, turning the prawns once more.

Serve the prawns with the butter from the pan and the burnt lemons on the side. Any unused butter can be wrapped and frozen for up to 1 month.

YAM PANCAKES WITH SMOKED MACKEREL AND HORSERADISH CREAM

African nutmeg or calabash nutmeg is also called ehuru, ehu, ariwo, awerewa, ehiri, airama or Jamaican nutmeg. It comes from evergreen forests of West Africa, specifically from the tropical tree *Monodora myristica*. It was introduced to Jamaica and parts of the Caribbean in the 18th century during the slave trade. You must only use a tiny bit because it is potent.

FOR THE YAM PANCAKES

175g (6oz) yams, skinned, cut into cubes (weight shown is the prepared weight)

1 large egg, beaten

50g (1³⁄₄oz/6 tbsp) self-raising flour

50g (1³⁄₄oz) potato flour or yam flour

½ tsp baking powder

125–150ml (4–5fl oz/½ cup–scant ⅔ cup) whole milk

pinch of freshly grated African nutmeg or calabash nutmeg

2–3 tbsp sunflower oil

salt and freshly ground black pepper

FOR THE HORSERADISH CRÈME FRAÎCHE

120g (4¼oz) full fat crème fraîche

1 tbsp good-quality horseradish cream

TO SERVE

2 smoked mackerel fillets

handful of finely chopped chives

4 sprigs of dill

Put the yam cubes in a saucepan of salted cold water and bring to the boil. Turn the heat down to a simmer, cover with the lid and cook until a knife inserted into the yam flesh passes through easily, 10–15 minutes. Drain, mash thoroughly and cool.

Put the mashed yams in a bowl, add the egg, both flours and the bicarbonate of soda (baking soda). Mix well to combine. Gradually add the milk, whisking until a smooth paste is formed (you may not need all the milk). Add the nutmeg and season with salt and pepper.

Preheat the oven to low (140°C/120°C fan/275°F/gas mark 1).

Heat ½ tablespoon of the oil in a non-stick pan and spoon about 2–3 tablespoons of the batter into the hot pan. The pancake should be thick. Cook for a couple of minutes until golden brown on the bottom. Carefully turn over and cook on the other side until golden brown. Remove from the pan, drain on a baking sheet lined with paper towels and keep warm in the oven while you cook the remaining pancakes, adding oil as needed. You should have enough batter for 4–6 pancakes.

For the horseradish cream, whisk the crème fraîche and horseradish together in a small bowl.

To serve, warm the mackerel fillets in the oven according to packaging instructions. Serve the pancakes topped with large flakes of the warm smoked mackerel and dollops of horseradish crème fraîche, garnished with chives and dill.

FONIO AND CASHEW NUT SODA BREAD

As I write this, it is indeed a coincidence that I am on the island of Ireland, the country to which soda bread is most famously attributed to. However, it was actually first created by Native Americans. They were the first to be documented using pearl ash, a natural form of soda formed from ashes of wood, to leaven their bread without yeast. The Irish adopted this technique in the 1830s, and now I am mixing up the ingredients with my West African-inspired produce – notably that 'supergrain' fonio, and cashew nuts. As it happens, Africa grows most of the world's raw cashews.

olive oil, for greasing

300g (10½oz/2¼ cups) wholemeal (whole wheat) flour

60g (2¼oz) fonio (see page 243)

100g (3½oz) salted cashew nuts, roughly chopped

1 tsp bicarbonate of soda (baking soda)

1 tsp baking powder

250ml (9fl oz/1 cup plus 2 tbsp) buttermilk

380–435ml (13–15¼fl oz/scant 2 cups) warm water

Preheat the oven to 200°C/180°C fan/400°F/gas mark 6. Lightly grease a 900g (2lb) loaf tin (loaf pan) with olive oil.

Put the flour, fonio, cashew nuts, bicarbonate of soda (baking soda) and baking powder in a large mixing bowl. Mix well and make a well in the centre.

Pour the buttermilk and water into the well and combine quickly using a wooden spoon. You may want to add the water gradually, to get the right consistency – the batter needs to be wet enough to allow the fonio to cook (this is more of a drop dough, rather than a dough you roll out). Spoon the dough into the prepared tin and bake until risen and golden on top, 35–40 minutes (keep a close eye on the bread as it bakes, ensuring it doesn't brown too quickly).

Remove the tin from the oven and leave to cool before turning out. Slice and serve with butter (I like mine with garlic or herb butter).

The bread will stay fresh for up to 2 days in an airtight container.

JAKATO FRITTERS WITH SPICY TOMATO SAUCE

Bitter balls, garden eggs or jakato, as it is commonly known in Freetown, is a fruit from the African garden aubergine (eggplant) called *Solanum aethiopicum*. It is low in sodium, low in calories and very high in dietary fibre. A slightly sweet, tender fruit covered with a shiny skin, it is often used in savoury dishes.

FOR THE JAKATO FRITTERS

400g (14oz) small jakato, sliced

1 tbsp salt

2–4 tbsp olive oil

1 medium onion, chopped

125g (4½ oz) halloumi cheese, grated

2 tbsp finely chopped parsley

1 tbsp finely chopped mint

2 cloves garlic, grated

½ tsp ground cumin

½ tsp sweet paprika

¼ tsp West African Pepper Blend (see page 23) or black pepper

60g (2¼oz) panko breadcrumbs

50g (1¾oz) plain (all-purpose) flour

sunflower oil, for deep frying

salt and pepper

FOR THE SPICY TOMATO SAUCE

400g (14oz) can chopped tomatoes

200ml (7fl oz/scant 1 cup) vegetable stock

Salone Fire Chilli Sauce (or chilli sauce of your choice)

large pinch of sugar

Put the jakato in a sieve (strainer), sprinkle over the 1 tablespoon of salt and mix with your hands. Set aside to disgorge (draw out the bitter juices) for one hour in the fridge.

Meanwhile, prepare the tomato sauce. Put the tomatoes and stock in a large pan over high heat. Bring to the boil then simmer, uncovered, stirring occasionally, until the sauce is thickened and reduced by half, 15–20 minutes. Add the Salone Fire chilli sauce and sugar and stir well. Taste, adjust the seasoning and set aside.

Preheat the oven to 240°C/220°C fan/475°F/gas mark 8.

Rinse the salt off the jakato, drain and pat dry with paper towels. Arrange in a single layer on a baking sheet and drizzle over the olive oil. Bake for 30 minutes or until the jakato is soft and slightly charred.

Allow to cool slightly, then transfer to a food processor along with the remaining fritter ingredients and whizz to a paste. Season with salt and pepper and form into 6–8 small fritters. Chill the in the fridge for 30 minutes to firm up.

When 30 minutes are up, heat the oil for frying in a deep, heavy-based pan no more than half full. To test if the oil is hot enough, drop a small breadcrumb into the hot oil. It should sizzle turn brown in 20 seconds.

Working in batches fry the jakato fritters until nicely golden, 5–10 minutes depending on size. Remove using a slotted spoon and drain on a baking sheet lined with paper towels. Serve the fritters with the spicy tomato sauce for dipping.

ROAST BONE MARROW WITH COCONUT AND PEANUT SAUCE AND SPICED BUTTER FLATBREADS

Bone marrow has been described as 'poor man's foie gras'. When spread on crispy, chewy, savoury flatbread – such as the one here – its intense flavour perfectly complements the rich peanut and coconut sauce. It's interwoven with a slight sweetness and a touch of spice: a truly luxurious dish and a treat for the senses. Incidentally, ghee is called cow butter in Sierra Leone.

You will need to begin the flatbreads and soak the bone marrow the day before serving.

FOR THE ROAST BONE MARROW

2 beef marrowbones, each cut into 3 x 5–6cm (2–2½in) pieces (ask your butcher to do this for you)

4 tsp sea salt

1 litre (35fl oz/4 ⅓cups) cold water

FOR THE FLATBREADS

400g (14oz/3 cups) plain (all-purpose) flour, plus extra for dusting

1 tsp salt

200ml (7fl oz/scant 1 cup) water

coconut oil, for brushing

FOR THE SPICED BUTTER FILLING

6 tbsp ghee

½ tsp ground cumin

½ tsp ground coriander

½ tsp West African Pepper Blend (see page 23)

FOR THE COCONUT AND PEANUT SAUCE

2 tsp cumin seeds

¾ tbsp coriander seeds

3 tbsp coconut oil

450g onions (about 2 large), finely chopped

20g (¾oz) garlic, grated

20g (¾oz) ginger, grated

1–2 scotch bonnet chillies, seeds left in, to taste

½ tsp West African Pepper Blend (see page 23)

1 tsp curry powder

75g (2½oz) no-salt smooth peanut butter (use one without palm oil)

2 medium tomatoes, chopped

35g (1¼oz) tomato paste (purée)

400ml (14fl oz) can coconut milk

1 tsp coconut sugar

1 litre (35fl oz/4 ⅓ cups) beef stock

salt

Continued overleaf

Soak the bone marrow overnight in the cold salted water (the fridge is ideal) to remove any impurities.

For the flatbreads, sift the flour into a large mixing bowl and make a well in the centre. Add the salt and water and mix to form a rough dough. Turn the dough out onto a floured work surface and knead for 10 minutes or until the dough is smooth and elastic. Cover with a clean dish towel and leave to rest for 10 minutes.

Meanwhile, for the spiced butter filling, melt the ghee in a small pan. Add all the spices, mix well then set aside to cool to room temperature.

Divide the rested dough into 6 equal balls. Working with one dough ball at a time (keep the rest covered as you work) roll out the dough balls on a floured work to a paper-thin circle.

Spoon 1 tablespoon of the spiced butter over the circle and spread it out carefully, leaving a small gap around the circumference. Gently roll the dough circle into a long thin log. Coil each end of the dough inwards until they meet in the centre, then fold the two coils into each other and press firmly into a swirl shape. Repeat with the remaining dough balls. Transfer the swirls to an oven tray, cover with clean dish towels and leave to rest for 20 minutes in the fridge.

For the coconut and peanut sauce, toast the cumin and coriander seeds in a dry frying pan until aromatic then grind to a powder in a pestle and mortar or spice grinder.

Heat the coconut oil in a saucepan, add the onions and fry gently, stirring occasionally, until golden brown and caramelized, about 15 minutes (don't rush this step). Add the garlic, ginger and chillies and cook for 2–3 minutes. Add the ground cumin and coriander mix, West African Pepper Blend and curry powder. Cook, stirring, for a further 2 minutes.

Add the peanut butter, tomatoes, tomato paste (purée), coconut milk, coconut sugar and beef stock. Bring to a boil, reduce the heat and simmer for 45 minutes or until the sauce is nice and thick. Taste and adjust the seasoning.

To finish the flatbreads, on a floured work surface roll each coil of dough into a circle of about 20cm (8in). Brush a non-stick pan with coconut oil and put the pan over medium heat. Cook each flatbread on one side until golden then carefully turn over and cook on the other. Each bread should take about 5 minutes in total to cook. Continue until all the flatbreads are cooked. Keep warm.

For the bone marrow, preheat the oven to 240°C/220°C fan/475°F/gas mark 8. Drain the marrow, put in a small roasting tin and roast for 15–20 minutes.

To eat, taking a piece of flatbread, dip in the peanut and coconut sauce and spoon over the bone marrow. Enjoy!

BLACK-EYED BEAN FRITTERS WITH YOGHURT, MAYO AND HARISSA SAUCE

Black-eyed beans (also known as binch) are indigenous to the African continent and are a staple food. Black-eyed beans, mung beans and red kidney beans are the most commonly used types of bean, used in soups, stews, rice dishes, salads and eaten as snacks. The beans are mostly grown on a small scale in compound gardens. Here I am using them to make a tasty fritter snack.

FOR THE YOGHURT, MAYO AND HARISSA SAUCE

3 tbsp Greek yoghurt

3 tbsp good-quality mayonnaise

2 tsp harissa paste

salt and pepper to taste

FOR THE FRITTERS

800g (1lb 12oz) cooked black-eyed beans (you could use 2 x 400g/14oz tins or soak and boil 400–450g/14oz–1 lb of your own beans)

1 bunch spring onions (scallions), finely chopped (about 8)

4 medium eggs

6 tbsp full-fat milk

2 tsp baking powder

70g (2½oz/½ cup) plain (all-purpose) flour

4 tsp harissa paste

6 tbsp olive oil

salt and pepper, to taste

For the yoghurt, mayo and harissa sauce, combine all the sauce ingredients in a bowl and mix well to combine. Set aside.

For the fritters, mash half of the beans in a bowl using a potato masher. Add the rest of the ingredients except the oil (including the whole beans) to the bowl with the mashed beans and mix to combine.

Heat 2 tbsp of the olive oil in a large non-stick frying pan over medium heat. When the oil is hot, spoon 2 tablespoon dollops of the bean mixture into the pan. Cook for 2–3 minutes on each side until golden brown, turning carefully. Remove with a spatula and drain on a plate lined with paper towels. Add more oil and repeat with another batch until all are cooked. Keep them warm as you go.

Serve with the yoghurt, mayo and harissa sauce.

CASSAVA CHIPS WITH WHITE TRUFFLE OIL, PARMESAN AND SAFFRON MAYO

If you are not familiar with cassava, it is tuber with a waxy, bark-like outer skin and a starchy centre. Cassava was introduced to Sierra Leone (and Africa more broadly) by Portuguese traders between 1415 and 1600 when they dominated world trade. It is now cultivated in more than 40 countries across the continent.

Cassava is one of the major staple foods for Sierra Leoneans, second to rice. For many people in major cassava production districts of the country, it is the major staple. The most popular meals made out of it are gari and fufu, which are common in many West African countries. It can also be used to make Cassava Flatbreads (see page 124).

This recipe combines my beloved cassava with European ingredients, such as Parmesan and truffle. The flavour is every bit as good as potato chips, if not better, with just the right subtle hint of earthy truffle. They're crispy on the outside, tender on the inside, perfectly salted and mixed with Parmesan to take them over the top. A simply luxurious snack!

Note: Cassava should not be eaten raw in large quantities because it contains a naturally occurring cyanide that is toxic to humans. Soaking, fermenting and cooking cassava are processes that render the toxin harmless.

FOR THE CASSAVA CHIPS

1kg (2lb 4oz) cassava

1 tsp sea salt

60g (2¼oz) Parmesan, grated

sunflower oil, for deep frying

Parmesan shavings, to serve

3 tbsp white truffle oil

FOR THE SAFFRON MAYO

large pinch of saffron

2 tbsp hot water

300g (10½oz) good-quality mayonnaise

1-2 cloves garlic, finely chopped

To peel the cassava, cut the cassava crosswise into 5-8cm (2-3in) pieces. Using a sharp knife, cut lengthwise through the bark-like exterior and into the pink skin beneath. Place the tip of the knife under the skin to loosen it and pull off the skin and bark. Cut into chunky chip-sized pieces.

As you work, rinse the cassava and put the pieces in a large saucepan with cold water so it doesn't discolour. When all are cut to size, add the salt and bring the pan of water to the boil. Boil until the cassava pieces are tender when pierced with a knife, about 25 minutes.

Meanwhile, make the saffron mayo. Crumble the saffron threads into a small bowl and pour over the hot water. Let it steep for 10 minutes.

Stir the mayonnaise and garlic together in a bowl. Add the saffron water and stir to combine. Taste and season with salt.

When the cassava is tender, drain it in a sieve (strainer) and set aside until completely dry.

Heat the oil for frying in a deep, heavy-based pan no more than half full. To test if the oil is hot enough, drop a small breadcrumb into the hot oil. It should sizzle turn brown in 20 seconds.

Working in small batches so as not to overcrowd the pan, fry the cassava chips until nicely golden, 5–10 minutes per batch. Remove with a slotted spoon and drain on a baking sheet lined with paper towels.

Toss the friend cassava chips with grated Parmesan and the white truffle oil. Serve with the saffron mayo on the side.

FONIO WITH SPICED ROAST PUMPKIN AND PINE NUTS

Fonio is a West African 'superfood'. It's cultivated from two species of grass with small grains. It's extremely nutritious with a very favourable taste. It's gluten free and high in dietary fibre. The grains can be used to make porridge, bread and beer and it can be made into flour as well.

I often use it in salads and as an alternative to couscous or rice. In this dish it's combined with pumpkin, another well-known ingredient in Africa (and elsewhere around the globe). Pumpkin is also known for its nutritional value; it's high in beta-carotene, vitamins C and E, iron and folate. This dish is just packed full of goodness.

1 medium pumpkin (about 500g/1lb 2oz), peeled, deseeded and cut into small cubes

4 tbsp olive oil

1 tsp ground cumin

1 tsp ground coriander

1 tsp West African Pepper Blend (see page 23)

1 tsp sweet paprika

½ tsp sea salt, plus extra to season

300ml (10½fl oz/1¼ cups plus 1 tsp) vegetable stock

150g (5½oz) fonio

100g (3½oz) pine nuts, lightly toasted

1–2 red chillies, deseeded and finely chopped

4 spring onions (scallions), finely sliced

1 tbsp chopped parsley

3 tbsp chopped coriander (cilantro)

1 tbsp chopped mint

FOR THE DRESSING

1 tbsp lemon juice

2½ tbsp olive oil

1 tsp red wine vinegar or apple cider vinegar

pinch of caster (superfine) sugar

Preheat the oven to 220°C/200°C fan/425°F/gas mark 7.

Put the pumpkin cubes in a roasting tin, drizzle over 3 tablespoons of the rapeseed oil, sprinkle over the spices and salt and toss to coat. Roast until brown and soft, about 30–40 minutes. Remove from the oven and set aside to cool.

To cook the fonio, bring the stock to the boil in a saucepan. Add the fonio, lower the heat and cook until all stock has been absorbed, about 5–10 minutes (test it to make sure it's tender). Stir through the remaining rapeseed oil and fluff the fonio with a fork. Turn off the heat and set aside to cool.

For the dressing, combine the lemon juice, olive oil, vinegar and sugar together in a bowl and mix well.

Put the roasted pumpkin, pine nuts, chilli, spring onions (scallions), herbs and fonio in a big mixing bowl. Add the dressing and toss together. Taste and adjust the seasoning and serve straightaway.

YAM, LEEK AND PANCETTA CROQUETTES WITH AIOLI

It is a historical fact that yams were the most common African staple fed to enslaved Africans onboard ships bound for the Americas during the slave trade. The slave merchant John Barbot noted that 'a ship that takes 500 slaves must provide above 100,000 yams', or roughly 200 per person for the journey across the Atlantic. Yams are a starchy edible root of the *Dioscorea* genus and are used in many African dishes. It doesn't take much to transform them into a really fancy croquette dish, like this one.

FOR THE CROQUETTES

30g (2 tbsp) butter

1 large leek, white part only, finely chopped, rinsed and drained

750g (1lb 10oz) yams, skins removed, rinsed, cut into large even chunks (weight shown is the prepared weight)

2 egg yolks, lightly beaten

3 tbsp double (heavy) cream

100g (3½oz) pancetta, fried until crisp

100g (3½oz) Manchego cheese, grated

sunflower oil for deep frying

salt and freshly ground white pepper

FOR THE COATING

50g (1¾oz/6 tbsp) plain (all-purpose) flour

2 whole eggs, lightly beaten

200g (7oz) panko breadcrumbs

FOR THE AIOLI

2 egg yolks, at room temperature

4 roasted garlic cloves (roast the cloves in their skins at 180°C/160°C fan/350°F/ gas mark 4 for 30 minutes or until soft)

large pinch of English mustard powder

300ml (10½fl oz/1¼ cups plus 1 tsp) sunflower oil

juice of ½ lemon

salt

For the croquettes, melt the butter in a saucepan over low heat. Add the leeks, cover with the lid and leave to sweat gently until very soft but not coloured, 20–30 minutes. Set aside to cool.

Meanwhile, make the aioli. Whizz the egg yolks, roast garlic, mustard powder and a pinch of salt in a blender or food processor until the ingredients combine. Very slowly drip in the oil while the blender or processor is running, until it thickens. Add lemon juice to taste, season with salt and add a few drops of water to loosen if needed.

The aioli can be made ahead and kept in the fridge (or stored as leftovers) for up to 1 week in a screw-top jar.

For the croquettes, put the yam chunks in a saucepan of salted cold water and bring to the boil. Turn the heat down to a simmer, cover with the lid and cook until a cutlery knife inserted into yam passes through easily, 10– 15 minutes.

Drain the yams and mash thoroughly, preferably using a potato ricer. Beat in the 2 egg yolks and the cream, then add the cooked leeks, pancetta and grated cheese. Season with salt and white pepper. Leave until firm and cool enough to handle, then shape the mixture into 10–15 even-sized croquettes.

For the coating, prepare 3 bowls: one for the flour, a second for the 3 beaten eggs and a third for the panko breadcrumbs.

Dip each croquette in the flour, pat excess off, then coat in the eggs before dipping into the breadcrumbs. Set the croquettes aside on a plate until all are coated.

Preheat the oven to low (140°C/120°C fan/275°F/gas mark 1).

Heat the oil for frying in a deep, heavy-based pan no more than half full. To test if the oil is hot enough, drop a small breadcrumb into the hot oil. It should sizzle turn brown in 20 seconds.

Working in batches so as not to overcrowd the pan, fry the croquettes until nicely golden, 3–5 minutes per batch. Remove with a slotted spoon and drain on a baking sheet lined with paper towels. Keep warm in the oven until all are cooked.

Serve with the aioli for dipping.

MAKES 12

PLANTAIN AND FETA HAND PIES WITH OVEN-DRIED TOMATO SALSA

This tasty, kinda healthy, little appetizer can work for vegetarians, too. The idea is based on the meat pies that we have in Sierra Leone (pies filled with meat or fish are a very popular party food). I decided to use plantain for a different take on the pie. Sweet plantain with the salty feta and the salsa with its chilli kick just tops it off.

FOR THE OVEN-DRIED TOMATO SALSA

10 large ripe plum tomatoes, halved lengthwise and cored, seeds and juice removed

1 tsp sea salt

ground black pepper

1 tsp chopped oregano

6 tbsp olive oil

1 medium onion (about 200g/7oz), finely chopped

1 clove garlic, chopped

¼ tsp finely chopped scotch bonnet chilli

2–3 tbsp finely chopped coriander (cilantro)

FOR THE PIES

4 yellow plantains

30g (2 tbsp) butter

1 large onion (about 250g/9oz), finely chopped

400g (14oz) feta cheese, crumbled

150g (5¼oz/1 cup plus 2 tbsp) plain (all-purpose) flour, plus extra to dust

1–1½ tsp salt

sunflower oil for deep frying

Start with the tomato salsa. Preheat the oven to low (140°C/120°C fan/275°F/gas mark 1). Line a baking sheet with baking paper.

Arrange the tomatoes on the lined baking sheet, sprinkle over the salt, pepper and oregano and drizzle with 2 tablespoons of the olive oil. Allow the tomatoes to dry in the low oven for 3 hours until they are shrivelled around edges but are still plump in the centres.

Heat the remaining 4 tablespoons olive oil in a large pan (use one with a lid). Add the onions and cover, cooking over a gentle heat. Cook, stirring from time to time, until they are well softened and turning golden brown, 5–10 minutes. Add the garlic and chilli and cook for a further 2–3 minutes, stirring.

Chop the dried tomatoes and add to pan. Take off heat, taste the salsa and season to taste. Just before serving with the pies, warm the salsa through then add the chopped coriander (cilantro).

For the pies, preheat the oven to 180°C/160°C fan/350°F/gas mark 4.

Wash the plantain, put them on a baking sheet and roast in the oven (skin on) for 40–50 minutes until soft.

Continued overleaf

While the plantain is in the oven, melt the butter over a gentle heat in a large pan (use one with a lid). Add the onions and cover with the lid. Cook, stirring from time to time, until the onions are well softened and turning golden brown. This process can take up to 1 hour. Do not be tempted to rush this step, as the slow-cooked onions give this dish its flavour. Once the onion is ready, take off heat and set aside until cool. Transfer the cooled onions to a bowl, mix with the feta and set aside.

When the plantains are ready, let them cool. When cool enough to handle, peel away and discard the plantain skins. Put the plantain flesh in a food processer and pulse, being careful not to overwork the mixture; you don't want it to become too sticky and elastic.

Transfer to a mixing bowl and add the flour and salt and mix to form a smooth dough.

Wrap the plantain dough in cling film (plastic wrap) and chill for 1 hour. Divide into 10 equal portions, each weighing 50–55g (1¾–2oz), and cover with a clean dish towel while you work.

If you have a tortilla press, line it with cling film (plastic wrap) or baking paper, place each dough portion into it and press to flatten. If you don't have a tortilla press, dust your work surface with flour and roll each dough portion out using a rolling pin to a circle about 15cm (6in) in diameter. Fill with 2 tablespoons of the feta and onion mixture then use your fingers to seal the edges of the pie. Continue until all 10 portions are filled with feta mixture.

The pies can be made ahead up to this stage and wrapped in a floured dish cloth and refrigerated for up to 4 hours until ready to fry.

Preheat the oven to low (140°C/120°C fan/275°F/gas mark 1). Heat the oil for frying in a wok or a deep pan over medium to high heat (don't fill the wok more than half full). To test if the oil is hot enough, drop a small breadcrumb into the hot oil. It should sizzle turn brown in 20 seconds.

Working in small batches so as not to overcrowd the pan, fry the pies until nicely golden, 3–5 minutes. Remove using a slotted spoon and drain on a baking sheet lined with paper towels. Keep warm in the oven until all are cooked.

Serve the pies warm with the oven-dried tomato salsa.

SERVES 4

BEETROOT SALAD WITH GOAT'S CHEESE AND GRANOLA

This recipe is made using egusi. Egusi (also known by variations including agusi, agushi) is the name for the fat- and protein-rich seeds of certain cucurbitaceous plants (squash, melon, gourd) which, after being dried and ground, are used as a major ingredient in West African cuisine.

There's a bit of disagreement on whether the word is used more properly to describe the seeds of the colocynth (*Citrullus colocynthis*), those of a particular large-seeded variety of watermelon, or generically for the seeds of any cucurbitaceous plant. The characteristics and uses of all these seeds are broadly similar. Major egusi-growing nations include Mali, Burkina Faso, Togo, Ghana, Côte d'Ivoire, Benin, Nigeria and Cameroon.

FOR THE BEETROOT SALAD

4 small individual crottin goat's cheese (50–60g/1¾–2¼oz each)

small handful of thyme, leaves picked

3 tbsp olive oil, plus extra to drizzle

500g (1lb 2oz) uncooked baby beetroot, scrubbed and trimmed

1 bay leaf

50g (1¾oz) lamb's lettuce

50g (1¾oz) baby salad leaves

1 bunch mint leaves

salt and freshly ground pepper

FOR THE GRANOLA

50g (1¾oz) fonio

3 tbsp egusi

1 tbsp sesame seeds

70g (2½oz) walnuts, roughly chopped

pinch of salt

1½ tbsp honey

1 tbsp water

drizzle of olive oil

FOR THE DRESSING

½ tsp Dijon mustard

¼ garlic clove, finely sliced

½ tsp chopped tarragon

1 tbsp champagne vinegar

4–5 tbsp olive oil

lemon juice to taste

Preheat the oven to 150°C/130°C fan/300°F/gas mark 2.

Cut each cheese in half horizontally and put in a bowl. Finely chop enough thyme to give 2 teaspoons and stir it into the 3 tablespoons olive oil. Pour this marinade over the goat's cheese and set aside.

For the granola, combine the fonio, egusi, sesame seeds and walnuts in a bowl with the salt. Heat the honey and measured water in a small pan until the honey is loosened then pour it over the ingredients in the bowl along with a drizzle of olive oil. Mix well, then spread out in a single layer on a baking sheet and bake until golden brown, 20–25 minutes. Leave to cool and set aside.

Spread the beetroot out onto a baking sheet lined with foil, drizzle olive oil, add a splash of water, the remaining thyme leaves and the bay leaf. Season generously with salt and pepper. Wrap in foil, seal and cook for 1–2 hours or until tender. Check the tenderness with the point of a cutlery knife. When the beetroot is tender, allow to cool a little then rub off the skins and cut into bite-size pieces.

To make the dressing, mix the mustard, garlic, tarragon and vinegar together in a bowl and season with salt and pepper. Whisk in the olive oil, taste and adjust the seasoning, adding lemon juice to balance the flavours.

Marinate the beetroot in half of the dressing for up to 24 hours before serving.

When you are ready to serve, heat the grill (broiler) to its highest setting. Place the goat's cheese on a baking sheet, season with pepper and grill (broil) until hot.

To serve, scatter the lamb's lettuce and baby leaves over the plates. Arrange 2 halves of goat's cheese on each plate and spoon over the beetroot and granola where there are gaps. Finish with the mint leaves and drizzle over the remaining dressing.

AFRO-FUSION MAINS

WHY AFRO-FUSION
COOKING RESONATES
WITH ME

Food fusion, at its core, is about taking in influences, ingredients and cooking methods from different continents, countries and cultures. Early explorers exchanged and combined food knowledge, and as they did so, inevitably recipes would become more complex and interesting. The fusion of culinary techniques and recipes has been in existence since the dawn of international trade and is all part of our planet's migration story.

The movement of people to and from Africa fascinates me. As a migrant myself, I am sometimes aghast at the way migrants are clumsily described in the mainstream media. Populism defines our current political age, and migration is a pressing contemporary issue. I believe that migration history should be placed at the heart of our national stories if it is to be more widely understood. It has shaped who we are – as individuals, as communities and as countries.

As a proud Sierra Leonean, Black African migrant, wife to a white British husband (that's the box he ticks on forms), and mother to mixed-race children, who travelled from Africa, to Kent, England, this history, this journey, has shaped me and my cooking. Food is a lens for culture, and you have to taste culture to understand it.

With my cooking, I try to celebrate Sierra Leonean food in a style more akin to fine dining and I've never seen that as hypocritical or as part of an attempt to fit into a European mainstream aesthetic. For me, using traditional techniques and flavour combinations, and enhancing or amplifying them with the finest quality ingredients is a tribute to those origins.

Afro-fusion is also misunderstood. Mixing techniques and flavours aids diversity, and its richness brings opportunity for creativity and innovation. It's a chance to push boundaries, explore new things and cross borders. I make no apology for bringing the reinvention of African dishes and ingredients to a broader audience and offering a whole new world of flavours to those who seek them out.

WHY AFRO-FUSION, WHY FREETOWN?

The Sierra Leone River, with a natural harbour at its mouth where Freetown now stands, is one of the places where slaving ships from European nations regularly docked to trade with local rulers for their transatlantic cargo, moving African people against their will to the Caribbean and Americas. It was also the site selected by British abolitionist Granville Sharp as a place to resettle freed salves.

In the 1780s, the number of freed slaves living in London was growing. The question was where they should best live and be employed, and the answer was that they should settle

WHEN I SOURCE INGREDIENTS, PREPARE FOOD, CURATE THE DINNING SPACE AND THE AMBIENCE AND WELCOME GUESTS, I AM INVITING THEM INTO MY LIFE.

in the continent from which they or their ancestors came. The first to arrive back from London, in 1787, came on a naval vessel carrying 331 freed slaves, 41 of them women, and – somewhat confusing the issue – 60 white London prostitutes. Looking back on this now, it is hard to understand how this was ever conceived of as a humane act.

Black settlers who had liberated themselves from American slavery were brought over from Nova Scotia and built a new settlement, named Freetown. In 1800, Maroons – free Black people from Jamaica – were also brought in. After the Act of Parliament of 1807 prohibited the slave trade in the British Empire, the British government took over the settlement on January 1 1808 as a naval base against the slave trade and as a centre to which slaves, captured in transit across the Atlantic, could be brought and freed. Between 1807 and 1864, when the last slave ship case was adjudicated in the Freetown courts, the British navy brought in more than 50,000 'recaptives,' also known as 'liberated Africans.'

The recaptives and their children, known as Creoles (today usually rendered Krios), prospered as traders, and some entered the professions, qualifying in Britain as doctors and lawyers. Thus, they formed an educated West African elite. Lebanese immigrants first came to West Africa in the mid-19th century, on boats headed for South America, and were known as 'Corals' because of their association with selling coral beads. Many Lebanese people remain in Sierra Leone today, running shops, hotels and businesses, and are proud Sierra Leoneans. They speak Krio and have become very much part of our community, making food like kibbeh (Lebanon's national dish) popular in Freetown.

HOW DOES THIS UNIQUE HISTORY LINK TO FOOD FUSION?

When broken down to their core, many classic recipes owe their existence to a coming together of several influences, rather than a single source of origin, which is where the boundaries of food fusion can be blurred.

Afro-fusion is a form of cooking that combines contrasting culinary traditions or techniques from traditional African cooking, or native ingredients from the African continent with others from around the world into a single dish. I tend to use ingredients that are from my homeland and flavours that are familiar to me, then combine them with flavours I have encountered in Europe.

Food fusion is all about experimentation and finding the combinations that work. Traditional dishes can be prepared with

fine ingredients and plated beautifully, but they must not lose their authenticity. It's important that we cherish traditional dishes, and yet keep crossing borders, boundaries and build bridges, not walls, and that's why Afro-fusion cooking is culturally important.

WHAT AFRO-FUSION MEANS TO ME

My city, my home country and continent are as much a feature and influence to what I do as my great-grandmother, grandmother, mother and my own migration story. My modern family is a meeting of two cultures, and I am both proudly African and British.

Food is our own tradition, it's about honesty and identity. When I source ingredients, prepare food, curate the dinning space and the ambience and welcome guests, I am inviting them into my life. I am sharing what I love, and maybe a bit of my soul.

RACK OF LAMB WITH KANKANKAN CRUST AND HERITAGE TOMATO SALAD

Food is deeply rooted in memory, and certain foods have the ability to transport us back to the past and to special places. I think there's a part of my brain where food, taste and visual memories mash together.

This dish is inspired by a place in Freetown where meat vendors come out at night on the Old Railway Line, just behind the Youyi Building (Lodge). Cooking and eating it takes me straight back there, every time.

3 x 6-bone racks of lamb, French-trimmed (ask your butcher to do this for you)

salt and pepper

FOR THE KANKANKAN CRUST

150g (5½oz) unsalted butter, softened

6 tbsp Kankankan Spice Mix (see page 56)

10 tbsp fresh breadcrumbs

handful of finely chopped fresh mixed herbs such as parsley, chives and thyme

1 tsp salt

FOR THE HERITAGE (HEIRLOOM) TOMATO SALAD

1 tbsp white wine vinegar

3 tbsp olive oil

½ tsp caster (superfine) sugar

2 shallots, chopped as finely as possible

1–2 tarragon sprigs, leaves finely chopped

500g (1lb 2oz) ripe heritage tomatoes, as many colours, shapes and flavours as you can get your hands on

salt and pepper to taste

For the kankankan crust, mix the butter, Kankankan Spice Mix, breadcrumbs and finely chopped herbs together in a bowl and mix well.

Season the lamb with the salt. Press a thin layer of the crust mixture over the rounded side of the lamb racks and place them in a shallow roasting tin. Chill for 30 minutes in the fridge to firm up the crust.

Preheat the oven to 220°C/200°C fan/425°F/gas mark 7.

Roast the lamb for 20–25 minutes, then remove and leave rest for about 10 minutes.

Meanwhile, for the tomato salad, whisk together white wine vinegar, olive oil, sugar and salt and pepper to taste. Add the shallots and tarragon and mix well.

Slice the tomatoes and arrange in a single layer on a large platter, mixing different colours and sizes. Check the seasoning of the dressing and adjust if needed.

To serve, slice the rested lamb into individual ribs and arrange on 6 plates. Pour the dressing over the tomatoes, making sure they are well coated, and serve.

SERVES 6

DUCK BREASTS WITH PUMPKIN, PEANUT AND COCONUT SAUCE

Peanut butter, pumpkin, coconut, duck breast and a whole lot of spices.
Another favourite packed full of flavour. Tender, moist, duck breast with
sweet pumpkin and a spicy sauce adding another level of yum.

6 duck breasts, trimmed of any sinew

FOR THE PUMPKIN, PEANUT AND COCONUT SAUCE

2 tsp cumin seeds

¾ tbsp coriander seeds

½ tsp curry powder

1 tsp West African Pepper Blend (see page 23)

3 tbsp coconut oil

2 large onions (about 450g/1 lb)

20g (¾oz) fresh ginger, grated

20g (¾oz) garlic (about 5 cloves), grated

1–2 scotch bonnet chillies, seeds left in, crushed to a paste

35g (1¼oz) tomato purée (paste)

200g (7oz) fresh tomatoes, chopped

1 tsp coconut sugar

75g (2½oz) unsalted smooth peanut butter (use one without palm oil)

400ml (14fl oz) can coconut milk

500ml (17fl oz/2 cups plus 2 tbsp) chicken stock

500g (1lb 2oz) pumpkin, peeled and diced

1–2 tsp salt or to taste

steamed fonio or coconut rice, to serve

Lightly toast the cumin and coriander seeds in a hot, dry frying pan until
aromatic. Grind in a pestle and mortar or food processor then mix with the
curry powder and West African Pepper Blend and set aside.

Heat the coconut oil in a large saucepan over medium heat. Add the onions and
cook gently, stirring, over low-medium heat until caramelized and very sweet,
about 30 minutes (don't be tempted to rush this step). Add the ginger, garlic and
chillies and cook, stirring, for about 5 minutes. Add the ground spices to the pan
and cook for a further 5 minutes on low heat, stirring.

Add the tomato purée (paste), chopped tomatoes, coconut sugar, peanut butter,
coconut milk and stock. Bring to a boil, taste and season. Add the pumpkin and
cook, stirring occasionally, until the sauce is thick and the pumpkin is tender,
20–30 minutes. Taste and adjust seasoning, then set aside. Just before serving with
the duck, warm the sauce through – add a splash of water if it's too thick.

Meanwhile, preheat the oven to 160°C/140°C fan/325°F/gas mark 3.

Pat the duck breasts dry using paper towels and use the tip of a sharp knife to
score the skin in diagonal lines about 3mm (⅛in) apart, being careful to cut only
the skin, not the flesh.

Season the duck breasts with salt and put them skin-side down in a cold ovenproof frying pan over low heat. This will allow the fat to render and the skin to slowly cook until golden and crisp. This process can take up to 10 minutes (make sure to keep the heat low). From time to time drain off the fat (save fat for making oven-roasted plantain).

Season the meat side with salt and pepper, flip the duck over and cook in the oven for 7–10 minutes depending on size of breast. The meat should still be pink. Rest the duck breasts for 3–5 minutes. Slice and serve with the warmed sauce and with fonio or Coconut Rice (see page 114).

SPICED ROASTED PLANTAIN WITH CONFIT CHERRY TOMATOES, SHALLOTS AND FETA CHEESE

This vegetarian dish is made with plantain, a member of the banana family. These fruits can be green, yellow or almost black, according to their ripeness. Cooked plantains are nutritionally very similar to a potato, calorie-wise, but contain more of some vitamins and minerals. They're a rich source of fibre, vitamins A, C and B6, and the minerals magnesium and potassium.

FOR THE CONFIT TOMATOES AND SHALLOTS

1 kg (2lb 4oz) mixed-colour cherry tomatoes

6 garlic cloves, finely sliced

¼ scotch bonnet chilli, finely chopped

12 baby shallots, peeled (halved if using larger shallots)

300ml (10½fl oz/1¼ cups plus 1 tbsp) olive oil

8 thyme sprigs

12 basil leaves

2 tsp sea salt flakes

ground black pepper

FOR THE SPICED PLANTAIN

6 yellow plantains, peeled and sliced in half vertically

1 tbsp coriander seeds

1½ tsp cumin seeds

2 tsp sweet paprika

1 tsp West African Pepper Blend (see page 23)

1½ tsp fine sea salt

6 tbsp olive oil

TO SERVE

250g (9oz) feta

handful baby coriander (cilantro) leaves

Preheat the oven to 110°C/90°C fan/225°F/gas mark ½.

Put the tomatoes in a large, deep baking tin, add the garlic, chilli and shallots, mix well and drizzle over the olive oil. Season with sea salt flakes and black pepper, then top with the herbs.

Roast for 2–2½ hours or until the shallots have become soft and sweet and the tomatoes have browned on top. Remove from the oven and set aside.

Turn up the oven temperature to 200°C/180°C fan/400°F/gas mark 6.

Put the sliced plantain in a roasting tin. Grind the whole spices in a pestle and morta or food processor, then mix with the paprika, West African Pepper Blend and salt. Rub the spices all over the plantains and drizzle over the olive oil. Roast for 25–30 minutes until the plantain is tender.

To serve, divide the plantain among 6 plates and top with the confit tomatoes and shallots. Crumble over the feta and garnish with baby coriander (cilantro) leaves.

FISH PEPE SOUP

This soup is spicy and light and many believe it to have medicinal qualities. All I know is it's the perfect morning-after-the-night-before dish that can take the place of paracetamol in curing a hangover.

4 snapper fillets (about 100g/3½oz each)

4 pak choi

salt and freshly ground black pepper

FOR THE SPICE BLEND

1 tsp black peppercorns

3 whole calabash nutmeg

10–13 (about 5g/⅛oz) pods grains of selim

1 tsp allspice berries

1 tsp grains of paradise

1½ tbsp coriander seeds

1½ tsp fennel seeds

1 tsp cloves

FOR THE SOUP BASE

3 tbsp olive oil

2 large red onions, finely chopped

25g (1oz) fresh ginger, finely chopped

3 cloves garlic, finely chopped

2 stalks lemongrass, finely chopped

1–2 scotch bonnet chillies, seeds left in, ground to a paste

4 tsp sweet paprika

70g (2½oz) tomato purée (paste)

110ml (3¾fl oz/scant ½ cup) white wine

2 litres (70fl oz/8¾ cups) good quality fish stock

300g (10½oz) haddock fillet, sliced

lemon juice, to taste

For the spice blend, lightly toast all the spices in a hot, dry frying pan until fragrant. Allow to cool, then grind in a pestle and mortar or spice grinder.

For the soup base, heat the olive oil in a large saucepan and, when hot, add the onions. Cook gently over medium heat until caramelized and sweet, about 30 minutes. Add the ginger, garlic, lemongrass and chillies and cook gently for 1–2 minutes. Add the 25g (1oz) of the spice blend (any left over will keep for up to 1 month in tightly sealed jar) and the tomato purée (paste) and cook, stirring, for 5–10 minutes. Add the wine, turn up the heat and cook until the liquid is reduced by half. Add the fish stock and sliced haddock, bring to a boil, then remove from heat and leave to infuse for about 1 hour.

When the time is up, blitz the soup base in a high-powered blender, then pass through a fine sieve (strainer) into a clean pan. Put the pulp from the sieve in a piece of muslin (cheesecloth) and squeeze as much of the liquid as you can back into the soup base. Taste and season with salt and lemon juice.

For the fish, prepare a steamer large enough to hold the fillets and pak choi in a single layer.

Season the snapper fillets and pak choi with salt and pepper and steam until they are cooked through and opaque, 5–10 minutes depending on thickness. Warm the soup through and serve it with the steamed snapper and pak choi.

OXTAIL PEPE SOUP

I love this soup for its winning combination of spice and comfort, and it's an excellent remedy when you're feeling sick or under the weather (self-induced or otherwise). You'll need to start this soup the day before you plan to eat it.

FOR THE SPICE BLEND

1 tsp black peppercorns

3 whole calabash nutmeg

10–13 (about 5g/⅛oz) pods grains of selim

1 tsp allspice berries

1 tsp grains of paradise

1½ tbsp coriander seeds

1½ tsp ground cumin

FOR THE SOUP

2kg (4lb 8oz) oxtail, chopped

salt

4 tbsp olive oil, plus extra as needed

2 large red onions, finely chopped

25g (1oz) fresh ginger, finely chopped

15g (½oz) garlic (about 6 cloves), finely chopped

1–2 scotch bonnet chillies, seeds left in, finely chopped

2–3 thyme sprigs

2 bay leaves

4 tsp paprika

70g (2½oz) tomato purée (paste)

100ml (3½fl oz/scant ½ cup) red wine

3 litres (105fl oz/13¼ cups) good-quality beef stock

200g (7oz) kale, trimmed

For the spice blend, lightly toast all the spices in a hot, dry frying pan until fragrant. Allow to cool, then grind in a pestle and mortar or spice grinder.

For the soup, season the oxtail with salt. Heat a drizzle of the oil in a large heavy-based pan (use one with a lid) over a medium-high heat. Working in batches so as not to crowd the pan, brown the meat all over, adding more oil as needed. Remove the meat using a slotted spoon and set aside, covered.

In the same pan, heat more oil if needed and add the onions. Cook gently, stirring, over a medium heat until caramelized and sweet, about 30 minutes. Don't be tempted to rush this step.

Add the ginger, garlic, chillies, thyme and bay leaves and cook gently for 1–2 minutes. Add the paprika, 25g (1oz) of the spice blend (any left over will keep for up to 1 month in tightly sealed jar) and tomato purée (paste) and cook, stirring, for 5–10 minutes. Stir in the red wine, using a wooden spoon to scrape any browned bits from the base of the pan, then allow to bubble for 2–3 minutes.

Return the meat to the pan and pour over the stock. Bring to the boil then reduce the heat to a gentle simmer. Cover with the lid and cook for about 3 hours or until the meat is tender and falling off the bone. Using tongs, transfer the meat to a plate and allow to cool. Shred the oxtail meat and discard the bones. Set aside.

Use a high-powered blender to blend the soup base until smooth, then pass it through a fine sieve (strainer) into a clean pan. Put the pulp from the sieve in a piece of muslin (cheesecloth) and squeeze out the remaining liquid into the soup base (discard the solids). Transfer all the liquid to a bowl, cover with cling film (plastic wrap) and leave in fridge (along with the shredded meat) overnight.

The next day, scrape away and discard the layer of fat on top of the soup. Prepare a steamer and steam the kale until tender, about 5 minutes. Spoon the soup (it will be nicely jellified) into a pan, heat through, taste and season. Warm the meat in a separate pan.

Serve the soup in bowls with the shredded oxtail meat and steamed kale leaves.

SERVES 8

CHICKEN SUPRÊMES IN PALM BUTTER SAUCE

A chicken suprême is a chicken breast with the wing bone still attached.
You may need to order them in advance from your butcher.

Many African recipes call for the fruit and oil of the African oil palm (*Elaesis guineensis*). Palm butter is made by boiling and grinding the palm fruit. It is a labour of love and requires time. Most cooks in the UK use ready-prepared tinned palm butter (also sold as palm cream or palm nut concentrate).

To prepare tinned palm butter for cooking, I empty the contents of the tin into a large bowl, add 1 litre (35fl oz/4⅓ cups) of hot water and then mix and strain the mixture through a sieve (strainer) several times to remove any chaff that remains from the pounded palm fruit. The resulting liquid is then used for cooking. It has a rich red colour and gives a silky, buttery richness to cooked dishes.

8 chicken suprêmes

salt

basil leaves, to garnish

FOR THE PALM BUTTER SAUCE

50g (1¾oz) dried smoked fish,
    available from African and Asian shops
    (see note on page 245), or dried anchovies

1 tbsp coriander seeds

1 tbsp cumin seeds

4 tsp sweet paprika

1 tbsp curry powder

1 tbsp West African Pepper Blend
    (see page 23)

400g (14oz) can palm butter/cream
    (often sold as palm nut concentrate)

1 litre (35fl oz/4⅓ cups) warm water

3 tbsp sunflower oil

3 red onions, finely chopped

30g (1oz) fresh ginger, finely chopped

15g (½oz) garlic (about 3 cloves), finely
    chopped

1–2 scotch bonnet chillies, seeds left in,
    crushed to a paste

70g (2½oz) tomato purée (paste)

100ml (3½fl oz) white wine

1 litre (35fl oz/4⅓ cups) chicken stock

250g (9oz) lightly smoked chicken, sliced

smoked salt

If you are using anchovies, soak them for about 30 minutes and rinse a couple of times with fresh clean water to get rid of the salt. Set aside. If you are using dried smoked fish, rinse and set aside.

For the palm butter sauce, lightly toast the coriander and cumin seeds in a hot, dry frying pan until aromatic. Grind to a powder in a pestle and mortar or food processor, combine with the paprika, curry powder and West African Pepper

Continued overleaf

Blend and set aside.

Combine the palm butter with the measured warm water in a large bowl, mixing well and making sure there's no grit or chaff in it (handle the palm butter carefully, as it does stain). Pass the mixture through a fine sieve (strainer) 2–3 times and set the liquid aside (discard the solids left in the strainer).

Heat the oil in a large heavy-based saucepan over low-medium heat. Add the onions and cook gently, stirring frequently, until they are caramelized and very sweet. This will take 15–20 minutes and mustn't be rushed.

Add the ginger, garlic and chillies to the pan and cook, stirring for a few minutes more, until softened. Add the spice mix to the onion mixture and stir well, making sure it doesn't stick to the bottom of the pan. Add the tomato purée (paste) and cook on low heat for 5–10 minutes.

Pour in the wine, turn up the heat and cook until the volume of liquid is reduced by half. Pour in the stock and about 500ml (17fl oz/2 cups plus 2 tbsp) of the palm butter liquid. (You can freeze any palm butter liquid left over for up to 3 months.) Add the fish and smoked chicken, bring to a boil then remove from the heat and leave to infuse for an hour or two.

After it's infused, transfer the mixture to a blender or food processor and blend until smooth. Pass the mixture through a fine sieve (strainer) in batches into a bowl. Transfer the solids from the sieve to a piece of muslin (cheesecloth) and squeeze as much liquid as you can into the bowl.

Return the sauce to a clean pan, season to taste and set aside until ready to use.

For the chicken suprêmes, heat the oven to 120°C/100°C fan/235°F/gas mark ½–1. Heat two large non-stick ovenproof frying pans over medium heat.

Season the chicken suprêmes on both sides with salt and place them skin-side down in the hot pans. Turn the heat to low, allowing the fat beneath the skin to render and the skin to become golden and crisp. This process can take up to 10 minutes. It's important it's done on a low heat or the skin will burn. Once the suprêmes are crisp and golden on the skin side, turn them over, transfer to the oven and cook for 15–20 minutes or until cooked through. Check by cutting down to the bone. If the juices run clear, it's cooked.

Serve the suprêmes with the warmed palm butter sauce and garnish with fresh basil leaves.

SERVES 5

BRAISED BEEF SHORT RIBS IN PEANUT AND COCONUT MILK

The coconut is a truly tropical fruit, which spread on its own to tropic coastal zones all over the world. The flesh and milk from coconuts are widely used in African cooking in relishes, sauces, desserts – you name it. Fresh coconut is sometimes peeled into slivers and used as topping for desserts. Coconut milk is widely used in all kinds of dishes. Creamed coconut comes in hard blocks and is used grated onto casseroles or used to make coconut milk by dissolving it in boiling water.

Coconuts are sometimes grown on plantations, but they are mostly harvested directly from wild trees. Did you know the name comes from the old Portuguese and Spanish word *coco*? This word means 'head' or 'skull'. The shell of the coconut also has three indentations, which resemble human facial features.

5 beef short ribs

2 tbsp sunflower oil

steamed coconut rice or fonio, to serve

salt

FOR THE PEANUT AND COCONUT SAUCE

2¼ tsp cumin seeds

¾ tbsp coriander seeds

1 tsp West African Pepper Blend (see page 23)

¾ tbsp curry powder

3½ tbsp coconut oil

2½–3 large onions (about 720g/1lb 9½oz), finely chopped

25g (1oz) garlic, grated

25g (1oz) ginger, grated

1–2 scotch bonnet chillies, seeds left in, finely chopped

45g (1½oz) tomato purée (paste)

250g (9oz) fresh tomatoes, chopped

½ tsp coconut sugar

300ml (10½fl oz/1¼ cups plus 1 tbsp) coconut milk

3 bay leaves

3 thyme sprigs

100g (3½ oz) unsalted smooth peanut butter (use one without palm oil)

500ml (17fl oz/2 cups plus 2 tbsp) beef stock

Preheat the oven to 150°C/130°C fan/300°F/gas mark 2.

For the sauce, lightly toast the cumin and coriander seeds in a hot, dry frying pan until aromatic. Grind in a pestle and mortar or food processor, combine the with the West African Pepper Blend and curry powder and set aside.

For the short ribs, heat the sunflower oil in a large frying pan over high heat. Season the short ribs with salt and add to the hot pan, frying on each side until golden brown, turning regularly. The aim here is not to cook them but to sear them and add flavour. Make sure to brown them well all over, then remove and set aside.

For the sauce, heat the coconut oil in a large heavy-based casserole or Dutch oven (use one with a lid). Add the onions and cook gently over low-medium heat until caramelized and very sweet. This will take up to 30 minutes and it's important not to rush this process. Add the garlic, ginger and chillies and cook, stirring, for 5 minutes more. Add the spices and cook for a further 5 minutes on low heat, stirring to prevent sticking.

Add the tomato purée (paste), chopped tomatoes, coconut sugar, coconut milk, bay leaves, thyme sprigs, peanut butter and beef stock to the pan. Stir well to combine, bring to the boil then add the short ribs to pan, making sure they're all covered by the sauce.

Cover with the lid and cook in the oven for 4–5 hours or until the meat is tender and falling off the bone. Remove from the oven, taste and add salt if needed. Serve with steamed coconut rice or fonio.

SPICED DUCK LEG CONFIT IN PEPE SOUP BROTH

Down at Moyamba Junction in Sierra Leone they do goat pepper soup, which is really tasty. My friend's husband also hunts whistling ducks in Sierra Leone and so, while this recipe is not what we could call a traditional Sierra Leonean main, it can be made in Freetown, or anywhere else in the world you can source similar ingredients.

You will need to start this recipe the day before you plan to eat it.

FOR THE SPICED DUCK LEG CONFIT

½ tbsp coriander seeds

1 tsp cumin seeds

1 tsp allspice berries

2 star anise

1½ medium cinnamon sticks

1 tbsp sea salt

2 garlic cloves

3 coriander (cilantro) sprigs, plus extra to garnish

2–2.5 litres (70–88fl oz/8–10½ cups) duck fat

6 duck legs

FOR THE PEPE SOUP BROTH

1 litre (35fl oz/4⅓ cups) good quality chicken stock

2 large red onions, sliced

25g (1oz) fresh ginger, sliced

15g (½oz) garlic (about 3 cloves), sliced

½–1 scotch bonnet chilli, deseeded and chopped

1 tbsp Pepe Soup Spice Blend (see page 102)

1½ tbsp oyster sauce

1½ tbsp Worcestershire sauce

1 tsp coconut sugar

1 lime (you may not need it all)

3 pak choi, cut in half

For the duck leg confit, toast the whole spices in a hot, dry frying pan over medium heat until fragrant. Grind to a paste in a pestle and mortar or food processor with the sea salt, garlic and coriander (cilantro).

Put the duck legs in a plastic bag, add the spice paste and rub it well into the duck. Leave to marinate overnight in the fridge.

The next day, preheat the oven to 150°C/130°C fan/300°F/gas mark 2.

Remove the duck legs from the bag, wiping off all the marinade. Put the duck legs in a single layer in a deep baking tin, pour over the duck fat to cover (heat it gently if it's not liquid) and cook in the oven for 3–4 hours or until the meat is tender.

Carefully lift out duck legs from the fat and trim off the knuckles. Place on an oven tray skin-side down.

Increase oven temperature to 180°C/160°C fan/350°F/gas mark 4. Put the duck legs on their tray back in the oven and cook for about 30 minutes. Turn the duck

legs skin-side up and cook for a further 10 minutes or until the skin is crispy. Set aside and keep warm.

For the broth, put the chicken stock in a saucepan and add the onions, ginger, garlic, chilli and Pepe Soup Spice Blend.

Bring to a boil and simmer gently on low heat for 30 minutes or until all the flavours are infused. Season the broth with oyster sauce, Worcestershire sauce, coconut sugar and the juice of ½ the lime. Taste and adjust seasoning, adding more lime juice if needed. The broth should be sweet, salty and spicy with plenty of flavour.

Strain the broth through a fine sieve (strainer) and discard the solids. Return the broth to the pan over medium heat. Add the pak choi and cook for 2–3 minutes until just tender.

To serve, divide the broth and pak choi among 6 bowls and top each with a confit duck leg, garnished with coriander (cilantro) sprigs.

SHWEN SHWEN BEEF STEW WITH COCONUT RICE

Sierra Leonean-style beef stew is but one component of a fabulous duet. Everyone knows Sierra Leone is the longstanding, undisputed heavyweight champion of the world when it comes to jollof rice, and this beef stew is its soul mate (or its match made in heaven). West Africans can get quite passionate about who makes the best jollof, and if the same rivalry existed for beef stew; it's safe to say we'd probably own that title, too. Passions run deep with this kind of talk so remember… I'm just joshing with you.

FOR THE BEEF STEW

1kg (2lb 4oz) stewing beef, cut into medium dice

250ml (9fl oz/generous 1 cup) sunflower oil, plus extra to drizzle

750ml (26fl oz/3¼ cups) beef stock

1¼ tsp coriander seeds

1 tsp cumin seeds

3–5 pods grains of selim

2 tsp sweet paprika

1 tsp West African Pepper Blend (see page 23)

20g (¾oz) fresh ginger

20g (¾oz) garlic (about 5 cloves)

1–2 scotch bonnet chillies, seeds left in, to taste

6–8 large onions (about1.5kg/3lb 5oz), finely chopped

55g (2oz) tomato purée (paste)

3 bay leaves

3 thyme sprigs

2 tsp salt

Jollof rice (see page 117), to serve

Heat a large heavy-based pan over medium-high heat. Season the diced beef lightly with salt just before browning.

Drizzle a little of the sunflower oil into the pan, using just enough to thinly coat the bottom. Cook the meat in batches so as not to overcrowd the pan and cause the meat to steam rather than fry. The meat should sizzle vigorously as it comes into contact with the pan.

Allow each piece of meat to brown thoroughly before moving it. Once browned underneath, it will release easily and can be turned to brown the other side. Brown the meat evenly on all sides but take care not to cook it any longer than necessary. Remove the browned meat from the pan and repeat the process until all the meat has been nicely browned.

Transfer the browned meat to a clean large saucepan and pour over the beef stock. Bring to the boil, turn down to a gentle simmer and cook until the meat is very tender but not quite breaking down, 60–70 minutes.

Continued overleaf

Meanwhile, toast the whole spices in a hot, dry frying pan until fragrant, then cool and finely grind in a pestle and mortar or food processor. Mix with the ground spices and set aside.

Blend the ginger, garlic and chillies to a paste in a food processor and set aside.

To make the stew, heat the 250ml (9fl oz/generous 1 cup) sunflower oil in a large, deep, heavy-based clean pan over medium heat. Add the onions, then dampen a piece of baking paper, flatten it out and lay it directly over the surface of the onions (this will prevent steam from escaping and will keep the onions soft as they cook). Turn the heat to low and cook over gentle heat, checking and stirring from time to time until the onions are well softened and turning golden brown. This process can take up to 1 hour and cannot be rushed – it is the gentle cooking of the onions and the caramelization that gives this stew its rich and slightly sweet flavour.

When the onions are soft and sweet, remove the paper, increase the heat and the add ginger, garlic and chilli paste. Cook for 1–2 minutes then add the spices, tomato purée (paste), bay leaves and thyme. Cook for another 1–2 minutes and add the meat without any liquid that may have accumulated during resting. It's very important that no liquid is added to the stew, because in Sierra Leone a 'stew' is not a liquid-based dish, so save the liquid to cook another dish. Season with 2 tsp salt or more to taste. Cook for a further 10 minutes, stirring gently a few times, on low heat. Remove and discard the bay leaves and thyme sprigs.

Serve the beef stew with Jollof Rice (see page opposite).

SHWEN SHWEN JOLLOF RICE

Jollof, or jollof rice, is a rice dish from West Africa. The origins of jollof rice can be traced to the Senegambian region that was ruled by the Wolof or Jolof Empire in the 14th century. Although these days most countries in West Africa have their own version of jollof rice, it is a widely accepted fact that Sierra Leonean jollof is the best in the whole of West Africa. Ask any Sierra Leonean and they will tell you that is true. However, this is not just any jollof. This is Shwen Shwen jollof and I have added in some additional spices.

1 tsp cumin seeds

1½ tsp coriander seeds

3–5 pods grains of selim

1 tsp West African Pepper Blend (see page 23)

2 tsp smoked paprika

1 tsp curry powder

15g (½oz) ginger

10g (¼oz) garlic (about 2 large cloves)

½–1 scotch bonnet chilli

100ml (3½fl oz/7 tbsp) sunflower oil

2 large red onions (about 500g/1lb 2oz), finely chopped

500g (1lb 2oz) basmati rice

200g (7oz) fresh tomatoes, chopped

35g (1¼oz) tomato purée (paste)

2 thyme sprigs

2 fresh bay leaves

500ml (17fl oz/2 cups plus 2 tbsp) beef stock warm, warmed

smoked salt

Toast the whole spices in a hot, dry frying pan until fragrant, then grind in a pestle and mortar or food processor. Mix with the ground spices.

Blend the ginger, garlic and scotch bonnet chilli to a paste in a food processor. Set aside.

Heat the oil in a large heavy-based pan with lid. Add the onions and cook on a gentle heat, stirring from time to time, until they are soft and golden brown, 20–30 minutes.

While the onions are cooking, put the rice in a large bowl, cover with cold water and use your hands to rinse the grains. Tip the water out and repeat 2–3 times until the water runs clear. Drain and set aside.

Add the ginger, garlic and chilli blend to the pan with the onions and cook for 2–3 minutes, turning the heat down if it starts to stick.

Add the spices to the pan and cook for a further 1–2 minutes, then add the chopped tomatoes, tomato purée (paste) and herbs. Cook for 3–5 minutes to get all the flavours to marry together, then add the drained rice. Stir well, making sure the rice is coated in the tomato base, for 5–10 minutes on gentle heat.

Continued overleaf

Add the stock a bit at a time, covering the pan between additions and cooking until all the stock has been absorbed. Check after 5 minutes and add more stock as needed. You want your rice to be cooked through but nice and fluffy. This process takes 30 minutes and cannot be rushed. When the rice is cooked but still a little al-dente, taste and season with smoked salt. Dampen a piece of baking paper then flatten it out and lay it directly over the rice (so no steam escapes). Cover with the lid and cook on a gentle heat for 20–30 minutes.

Leave it to rest for 10 minutes then discard the baking paper, bay leaves and thyme sprigs. Serve on its own or with Salone Fire Chilli Sauce if you need extra heat.

EBBEH WITH CURED MACKEREL AND CRISPY SWEET POTATO FRIES

This is a hearty, chunky, creamy, tropical root vegetable pottage, which I serve with cured grilled mackerel and crispy fries. Yams should not be confused with sweet potatoes. Yams have a white flesh and have a texture that's similar to a turnip. The flesh can be eaten boiled, roasted, baked, mashed or made into fries.

Cocoyam is a nutritious root vegetable that is eaten across the African continent. Growing up to 1.8m (6ft) tall, cocoyam is a large perennial plant with large heart-shaped leaves and turnip-sized corms (the edible part). Beneath the skin, the colour of its flesh varies from white to cream to yellow or purple, depending on the species and it has water chestnut-like nutty flavour.

This crop was first introduced to West Africa as far back as the 16th-17th centuries and travelled to the continent via the infamous middle passage to Africa. Its leaves can also be cooked as plasas (see page 138).

In Sierra Leone, we usually eat ebbeh on Fridays although it's not usually as elaborate as this version. I have added cured mackerel for extra protein. Needless to say, this root vegetable pottage is super healthy. Healthy is good, but to be honest, it's the comforting taste and texture that grab me. I think I like it on days two, three and four even better.

FOR THE POTTAGE

350g (10½oz) yam

350g (1lb 2oz) sweet potatoes

250g (7oz) cocoyam

250g (7oz) cassava

3 tbsp red palm oil

1 large onion, peeled and chopped

1–2 scotch bonnet chillies, seeds left in, to taste

1 tbsp sweet paprika

50g (1¾oz) dried smoked fish, available from African and Asian shops (see note on page 245), soaked in water to cover for 30 minutes and rinsed (optional)

1–1.5 litre (35fl oz–52fl oz/4 ⅓ cups–6½ cups) of chicken stock or vegetable stock.

1 bunch coriander (cilantro), finely chopped, plus extra leaves to garnish

salt and freshly ground black pepper

FOR THE CURED MACKEREL

300g (10½oz) fine sea salt

300g (10½oz) caster (superfine) sugar

2 tbsp fennel seeds, toasted in a hot, dry pan and ground in a pestle and mortar or spice grinder

2 tbsp coriander seeds, toasted in a hot, dry pan and ground in a pestle and mortar or spice grinder

8 large mackerel fillets

FOR THE CRISPY SWEET POTATO FRIES

500g (1lb 2oz) sweet potatoes

1 tbsp sunflower oil

Continued overleaf

For the pottage, peel all the root vegetables, cut them into bite-size pieces and put them in a large bowl of cool water to prevent discolouration.

In a large heavy-based pan, heat the palm oil over medium heat. Add the onions and cook gently, stirring, until soft and sweet, about 30 minutes.

While the onions are cooking, mix the salt, sugar and spices together for the cured mackerel. Lay the mackerel fillets flat in the base of a glass or ceramic dish. Sprinkle the curing mixture over the mackerel to cover evenly and leave to cure for up to 1 hour; you can cure the fish for less time (a minimum of 12–15 minutes), depending on how 'cured' you want your fish to be.

At the end of the curing time (the fillets will have firmed up), rinse the mackerel fillets under cold water to remove the curing mixture. Pat dry with paper towels and set aside, covered in the fridge, until just before serving.

Meanwhile, once the onions are ready, add the chillies, paprika and fish (if using), season with salt and cook, stirring, for about 5 minutes. Add 1 litre (35fl oz/4⅓ cups) of chicken stock to the pan and use a wooden spoon to scrape up all the browned bits from the base of the pan, then bring to a boil.

Add the yam, cassava, sweet potato and cocoyam. Cook, stirring frequently, until the vegetables are tender and starting to break down and the pottage is thickening, 30–35 minutes. Add more stock if needed. At the end of cooking, stir in the coriander (cilantro), taste and season with salt and freshly ground black pepper.

While the pottage is cooking, make the sweet potato fries. Preheat the oven to 220°C/200°C fan/425°F/gas mark 7. Line a baking sheet with baking paper.

Use a spiralizer to spiralize the sweet potato fries and place on them on the prepared baking sheet. Drizzle with sunflower oil and season with salt and pepper. Using your hands, mix the seasoning into the sweet potatoes so they are well coated. Bake for 20–25 minutes or until crispy, keeping an eye on them and turning once so they don't burn.

Towards the end of the cooking time for the sweet potato fries, heat the grill (broiler) to high. Grill (broil) the mackerel fillets for 2–3 minutes on each side. Serve the mackerel fillets on top of the pottage and garnish with coriander leaves and the sweet potato fries.

PLANTAIN FLATBREADS

Adding ripe plantain to a standard flatbread recipe gives it additional sweetness and softness.

1 black (ripe) plantain

300g (10½ oz/2 cups plus 2 tbsp) self-raising flour, plus extra for dusting

1 tsp baking powder

50g (1¾ oz/3½ tbsp) butter, melted (optional)

Bring a small saucepan of water to the boil.

Wash (but don't peel) the plantain, top and tail, cut in half widthways, then cut horizontally into thirds.

Put the plantain in a second saucepan, cover with the boiling water and bring back to the boil.

Boil the plantain halves in the saucepan with the skin on for 10–15 minutes until tender, then drain (reserve the cooking water) and leave to cool before peeling.

Blend the cooled, peeled plantain with 4 tablespoons of the cooking water in a food processor or blender until smooth.

Put the flour and baking powder in a mixing bowl, add the blended plantain and mix to form a dough. Knead the dough on a dusted work surface for about 5 minutes. You are aiming for a soft dough here. If it's too sticky, add a little flour or if it's too dry add a splash of cooking water.

Leave the dough to stand at room temperature for 30 minutes, then divide the dough into 10 even-sized balls.

On a lightly floured work surface, roll out the dough balls to circles of about 15cm (6in) diameter using a rolling pin. Roll the dough as thin as you can. Try not to use too much flour as you do not want to dry out the dough or make the breads heavy. Don't worry if the circles are not perfect. After all, our differences are what makes us unique.

Heat a dry frying pan over medium heat. Once hot, add a flatbread and cook for about 2 minutes on each side until they're puffed up, turning with tongs halfway through. Remove from the pan, brush with some of the melted butter (if using) and pile onto a banana leaf or plate. Keep warm while you cook the remaining flatbreads. Repeat until all are cooked. Serve the flatbreads warm.

KANKANKAN RIBEYE SKEWERS

In Sierra Leone, kankankan is sold wrapped in old newspaper, usually served with very hot cayenne pepper and thinly sliced onion. It's an all-time favourite, like fish and chips to British people. It's a Friday-evening, chilling-out-with-your-friends or going-out-clubbing feast.

Nightlife in Sierra Leone starts at about 11pm or midnight. It's not unusual for people to nap after work to get them in the mood for a weekend or a Friday night. To me, Freetown is the enjoyment capital. It's a great place to hang out in the evening time.

FOR THE KANKANKAN RIBEYE

2 ribeye steaks (about 250g/9oz each)

3 tbsp peanut oil

4–5 tbsp Kankankan Spice Mix (see page 56), plus extra to sprinkle

1 red onion, finely sliced

4 ripe heritage tomatoes or 2 handfuls colourful cherry tomatoes, thinly sliced

hot cayenne pepper for sprinkling (optional)

Use a sharp knife to cut the steaks into thin slices and put them in a bowl. Coat the meat strips liberally with the peanut oil and Kankankan Spice Mix until evenly coated, then season with salt.

Thread the steak slices onto metal skewers, making sure that the meat is a flat as possible. Sprinkle a bit more Kankankan Spice Mix over the meat and leave to rest at room temperature for 15–20 minutes.

Preheat the grill (broiler) or a barbecue and when it's good and hot, cook the meat for 2–5 minutes, depending on how you prefer it cooked, turning the skewers regularly to prevent the meat from burning.

When it's cooked to your liking, allow the meat to rest for about 5 minutes. Serve on an old newspaper with the sliced red onion and tomatoes, and cayenne pepper (if using).

CASSAVA FLATBREADS WITH ONION STEW WITH PAN-FRIED SEA BASS

Many Sierra Leoneans will relate to this recipe and, for me personally, I cannot imagine Sierra Leonean street food without this beloved dish of cassava flatbread, onions cooked slowly in coconut oil and spices and topped with fried fish (my version is made with pan-fried sea bass fillet). If you're travelling to the Provinces, you may stop at Waterloo Junction en route to Bo. If you do, be sure to pick up some *casada braid en fry fish* as it's called in Krio, Sierra Leone's Creole language. I tend to use sea bass but there is a wide variety of fish that can be used.

Note: Cassava should not be eaten raw in large quantities because it contains a naturally occurring cyanide that is toxic to humans. Soaking, fermenting and cooking cassava are processes that render the toxin harmless.

When making the flatbreads, it is best to use a 9–10cm (3½–4in) food ring to give each flatbread a nice circular shape. Once it's shaped, remove from the ring and flatten with the heel of your hand.

If you'd like to make this recipe to serve 6 people, just add 2 extra sea bass fillets.

FOR THE CASSAVA FLATBREADS

4 medium cassava (1.8–2kg/4lb–4lb 8oz lb, peeled, rinsed and grated

salt

FOR THE ONION STEW

180g (6oz/scant ¾ cup) cold-pressed coconut oil

3 large onions (about 750g/1lb 10oz), finely sliced

3–4 tsp Salone Fire Chilli Sauce (or chilli sauce of your choice) or to taste

15g (½oz) garlic

2g (⅛oz) fennel seeds, toasted and ground

15g (½oz) fresh ginger

2 tsp West African pepper mix

2½ tsp curry powder

1 tsp salt

2 tsp tomato purée (paste)

150g (5½oz) cooked brown shrimp (optional)

FOR THE PAN-FRIED SEA BASS

4 sea bass fillets (about 150g/5½oz each)

4 tbsp sunflower oil

salt and pepper

Continued overleaf

For the onion stew, melt the coconut oil in a large, heavy-based saucepan (use one with a lid). Add the onions, cover with the lid and cook over a gentle heat, stirring from time to time, until the onions are nicely softened and turning golden brown. This process can take up to 1 hour. Do not be tempted to rush this stage as the slow caramelization is what gives this simple dish its rich flavour.

Meanwhile, for the cassava flatbreads, put the grated cassava in a clean dish towel. Twist the towel and wring out over the sink to squeeze out as much liquid as you can. (If the cassava isn't completely dry, try drying it out on a clean dish towel.) Transfer to a food processor and blend until smooth. Season with salt.

Transfer the cassava to a bowl and rub the mixture with your fingertips, removing and discarding any remaining lumps. Pass through a sieve into a bowl (discard what's left in the sieve); the aim here is to achieve a fine granular consistency.

Heat a non-stick frying pan. When the pan is hot, drop the mixture in 2–tablespoon heaps into the pan (using a food ring makes it easier and gives them a nice shape). Remove the ring, if using, and flatten the bread using a heatproof spatula.

Cook on medium heat for 1–2 minutes, then carefully flip over and cook for 1–2 minutes further on the other side or until cooked through. The aim is not to give any colour; they should remain as white as possible.

Continue until all the cassava mixture is used up (you should have enough 15–20 flatbreads, 2 per person for a starter, 3 per person for a main), wiping the pan clean between batches. Keep the flatbreads warm under a clean tea towel.

When the onions are ready, increase the heat to medium and add the Salone Fire Chilli Sauce and all of the spices to the pan. Cook for 1 minute, stirring continuously. Add the tomato purée (paste) and reduce the heat to low. Cook for 2–3 minutes then take off heat. Stir in the cooked brown shrimp, if using. Set aside and keep warm.

For the sea bass, heat a heavy-based frying pan over high heat. When hot, add 2 tablespoons of the oil. Season the fish with salt and pepper and lay 2 fillets in the pan, skin-side down. Gently press each fillet down with a spatula to prevent it curling at the edges as it cooks.

Reduce the heat to medium then cook for 3–4 minutes further undisturbed, until you can see the flesh has cooked two thirds of the way up and the skin is crispy and brown.

Carefully flip the fillets over, then fry on the flesh side for about 2 minutes until just done. Leave to rest, skin-side up. Repeat the process with the two remaining fillets.

Serve the flatbreads topped with the onion stew, with the fish on top.

Note: Any leftover flatbreads can be frozen. Layer the flatbreads between sheets of baking paper and freeze in a resealable plastic bag. Defrost overnight in the fridge, then sprinkle the breads with water and reheat in a single layer in the microwave for 1 minute.

TRADITIONAŁ MAINS

THE HALFWAY

I was born at Lumley Hospital, in the western area of Freetown, on 17 March, 1981.
My childhood, although I don't remember much of it, was eventful. Here, now, writing this, I feel as if I'm walking along the bookshelves of some ancient untouched library. In there lies a particular book. It's heavier than any of the others and as I pull it out and wipe off the dust, it becomes more familiar. Each letter becomes clearer and each sentence more meaningful.

As I flick through its pages, I find reading this book much easier than I had imagined. There are extracts that are harshly cold and there are extracts that hold a warmth I could only dream to feel again and, in that moment, despite the bitter stings, I wonder why I had left the library so desolate in the first place. Feelings about the past like these are simply part of growing up. Forgiving what is forgivable and acknowledging what is not. It's what allows me to visit my library and accept it for what it is.

For the most part, I was very well behaved. My studies were very important to me, I did as my elders asked me to and I was very helpful around the house. However, there was one thing I did used to get in trouble for. Every once in a while, I would be caught stealing cooking utensils and ingredients from the kitchen, sneaking them off outside and making all sorts of bizarre concoctions. It was all part of a common childhood activity in Sierra Leone called 'play cook'.

I remember gathering dolls and pretending to feed them what I had made. Eventually, when the dolls' reactions weren't convincing enough, I began forcing other children to try my food as well – which unfortunately always seemed to end in tears. But to the few who would entertain me, harbouring food in their cheeks, forcing grimaces into grins and as generously giving me a few words of encouragement before retreating to spit out the poison I had fed them – I hold them in my heart with gratitude and endearment.

No one really works for the sake of working. Be it money, be it self-fulfilment, there is always some other motivation. For me, it was watching the reactions of others trying my food and the feeling that every cut I received from clumsy handling of the knife, every burn from the stove and every food stain on my clothing was a battle scar.

It was in those early, boundlessly sunny days, when we laughed until we cried and cried until we could finally laugh again, that this madness took root. Just as the pen will never be prised out of the hand that was born to write, or the podium be stolen from under the feet of a voice that was meant to be heard, I find myself always coming back to the kitchen. I'm fortunate that I've never been too far from my passion. From the age of nine, I would cook rice every day when I got home from school. My mother was very busy with work, so she

IT SEEMS THE MORE I RECALL MY CHILDHOOD, THE LESS I AM ABLE TO HOLD ON TO THAT 'ANGEL-CHILD' IMAGE I SEEMED TO HAVE PAINTED OF MYSELF BEFORE.

would make different sauces for the week and all I would have to do is make the rice, heat up the sauces and call everyone to eat.

It's all foggy now, but I remember we moved around a lot when I was younger. There was Wilkinson Road and Tengbeh Town in Freetown, then Bo. We were with my grandmother's sister for a while and then with my mother's cousin. This is where it clears up a little... Bo was very different than Freetown. I was six or seven at the time and the transition to my new school was difficult. However, if ever there was a ray of sunshine, it was my three siblings. The youngest is Rosaline, also known as Mama; the second-youngest is Isata, although friends and family know her as Kuku; and then my older brother, Bashiru.

My mother's cousin was a trader, and she often asked my siblings and me to sell produce for her in the market. It's not unusual for Sierra Leonean children to aid their family with work; in fact, it would be more unusual if they did not. Still, at such a young age and after long days at school, this work was taxing.

In Freetown I was never allowed to go up the market unattended and suddenly I found myself taking a basket of produce upon my head every day after school and pacing miles up and down the crowded streets. My mother's

cousin had a rule: if we were not able to sell all the produce she had given us before returning home, we would be punished.

It was a terrifying predicament, not only for me but for my little sister Kuku, who was only four at the time, and for Bashiru who was nine and carried the brunt of it was. Back then, everyone and everything felt unfamiliar and, after moving around so much, we concluded that it was the three of us against the world. Being the eldest, Bashiru had to grow up very quickly so that he could better protect my sister and me. Each day at the market, Bashiru worked twice as hard to sell all his produce and, as the foreboding grey of twilight crept over the humid streets, he lumbered everything that Kuku and I were unable to sell into his own basket and led the two of us home.

He'd always been like that; serious but kind-hearted and genuine. It seems the more I recall my childhood, the less I am able to hold on to that 'angel-child' image I seemed to have painted of myself before. You see, as a child I always had to have the last word. I must say, it did not go very far with adults, but with children my age and sometimes even older I certainly pushed my luck.

One day, when I was walking home from school with my brother, we ran into a group

of older boys. They were clearly no match for either of us but as they started to jeer and tease, I couldn't hold my tongue. I soon realised that this time I had really done it but before I could whisper my last prayers, Bashiru stood up for me. Begrudgingly, of course, and no doubt wondering what terrible thing he'd done in a past life to have me as a sister. That day he was beaten up, and they even stole his shoes! It's funny and endearing to think of now but I remember it was much less so then.

Our time with our mother's cousin was, luckily, very brief. As soon as news got back to my mother in Freetown of how we were being treated, she picked us up that very day and we soon got back to a sense of normality. Alas, in Freetown abnormality is normality. My life wasn't any easier before and wouldn't be any easier later on. The story I'm telling you is only a pebble in a mountain of other narratives that I could tell; but that's another book and I hope by what you have heard you can understand what I mean by 'warmth' and 'coldness' in these memories that I keep tucked away.

Moving to the UK was a highly emotional experience for me. I didn't grow up knowing my life might take me to another country, so it's not something I necessarily yearned for. Yet, when the opportunity arose, I knew I had to grasp it. I certainly felt the pressure of responsibility to come to the UK and succeed, and for many years the powerful emotion of guilt weighed very heavily on my shoulders. My feelings of guilt were strong and long-lasting as a result of leaving my family and loved ones back in Sierra Leone and trying to convey what I was experiencing in this new country wasn't easy. Life in the UK is good, but I spent many years pining to return home, or perhaps to return to a time when life was slower, simpler, less pressured and less complicated. It took me many years to truly settle.

Guilt is a powerful emotion that can often impact on the wellbeing of migrants and migrant families as they try to settle and build a life in a new country.

Cultural diversity is wonderful, but it can occasionally make communication difficult. Different cultures have different mindsets, different meaning of words, behaviours, gestures and tones of voice, and this plays out when trying to attain qualifications, progress a career and navigate the system. There are different attitudes to conflict, different attitudes towards disclosure and differences in decision-making. Migration is not a crime. It's not a one-directional process either. It's a colossal process that has been happening in all directions for thousands of years.

The first time I stepped foot on English soil was also the first time I had ever left Africa. As you can imagine, coming from a country where average temperatures ranged between 20–30°C (68–86°F), my first reaction was shock at how cold it was. No matter how much I had heard about the weather in Britain, nothing could've prepared me for that.

The second reaction is harder to explain. It was a lonely mix of uncertainty and apprehension. For the first time in my life, I was a complete stranger to the world; it was undeniable that I was different and there was no fitting in. I came to England on a student visa and my guardian lived in West Malling, in the county of Kent. If any you reading this are familiar with Kent, you will probably know that it isn't exactly multicultural. I didn't only feel different, I looked different. It was an obvious fact that I could not hide and because of it I was met with a number of uncomfortable experiences.

Once people had worked out where I was from, they would immediately ask about Sierra Leone's Civil War, which began in March 1991. To me, it wasn't good conversation. People has suffered greatly and at the time, I still suffered from nightmares. But they all had a sort of morbid curiosity about war that robbed them

of all rationality, empathy and understanding that, rather than just a news story, the war was a real tragedy that happened to real people. I believe that those experiences also helped fuel my desire to show Sierra Leone in a different light. There are many things about my country and its history that are horrible and twisted but at the same time there is so much that we must cherish and celebrate.

By the time I was 24, I was married and had given birth to my daughter, Charlie. I was working in accounting while my husband, Ben, was studying part-time. I had everything: a stable career and a loving family of my own, but I was plagued by the feeling of having nothing at the same time. Truth is, I hated accounting, but there wasn't really much else that I could do or wanted to do. Cooking

wasn't even a thought. You don't work that hard academically and travel six hours across the ocean to consider a 'hobby' as a career.

This confliction is probably a story all too familiar to many people – the classic immigrant paradox. I had become prisoner to the guilt of knowing that there were people back home who could only dream of the opportunities I had been given. Before I knew it, I was subconsciously chanting, 'Don't mess it up, don't mess it up' in my head every day. In the end, I learned that it is impossible to go on like that.

I didn't start cooking as a career until I was 34 or 35 (by which time I had also had my son, Chase). I began cooking for friends and families' events for small change, which

I'VE LEARNED THAT I HAD UNDERESTIMATED MYSELF ALL MY LIFE AND BREAKING FREE FROM THAT AND FINDING THAT I CAN DO SO MUCH MORE WITH MY COOKING IS A FEELING I COULD NOT PUT INTO WORDS.

eventually helped me build up enough confidence to advertise myself to wider audiences in the hope that I could build my passion into something more. Not to jinx anything but... it's going pretty well.

As I quickly use up what's left of my accounting skills, I can tell you that 34-24=10 and therefore I had been stuck in a profession that I hated for a decade. So, here's a little advice to any young creatives out there: follow your dreams but weigh your options. If you hate your job, it shows; it takes a toll not only your work performance but on your mental health. This being said, I do not want to tell you all to drop a well-paying job and join the circus just because you've got a sense of humour. Test the waters before you jump because you could end up scalding yourself, but never forget that life is longer than we think. Don't limit yourself to anything just because that's the road you set out on at the beginning.

I'm slowly but surely moving past age 40 now but learning every day and growing and nurturing my passion. I've learned that I had underestimated myself all my life and breaking free from that and finding that I can do so much more with my cooking is a feeling I

could not put into words. In a way, I feel as if I'm finally giving something back to the timid, unsure teenage me. Showing her that she has so much to be proud of about her heritage.

To me, Shwen Shwen is not just cooking. It is the preservation of traditions, proof that we can do so much more with our ingredients and cuisine and belief in a country that is too often looked down upon.

People are like Russian dolls; each year adds a new layer. Although I am in my 40s, I still feel 34 and am gaining more confidence in myself every day. I am realising that I have already wasted too much time being afraid. I still feel like a teenager who wishes to say all the things now that I couldn't say to those condescending eyes back then, and I still feel like a child who is loving cooking and creating more and more as the years go by.

SWEET POTATO LEAVES/PLASAS

Plasas to Sierra Leoneans is a category of food that describes leafy green sauces. We have quite a few. This is our Shwen Shwen, premier plasas. Plasas is always made with meat or fish, sometimes both, with dried/smoked fish and ogirie (fermented sesame seeds) for flavouring. We use thickening agents like peanut butter, egusi (melon seeds) and dried okra powder in some of them. They are quite a palaver to prepare, hence the name plasas, which comes from the Portuguese word *palaver* and dates back hundreds of years, possibly as far as the 13th century or further, but picked up by English sailors in the 18th century and then adopted into Krio. We also have palaver huts, which were tribal places used for arbitration or settling quarrels, disputes and negotiations. This dish is my taste of home.

100g (3½oz) ogirie (fermented sesame seeds)

2 tsp salt, plus extra to taste

1.5kg (3lb 5oz) goat meat on the bone, diced (you might be able to buy this frozen in 1kg/2lb 4oz bags in African shops)

1 litre (35fl oz/4⅓ cups) beef stock

300ml (10½fl oz/1¼ cups) red palm oil

1 aubergine, peeled and finely sliced (optional)

8 large jakato (garden eggs)

100g (3½ oz) dried smoked fish, available from African and Asian shops (see note on page 245), or dried anchovies

400g (14oz) onions (about 2 medium), finely chopped

400g (14oz) can butter beans, drained

800g (1lb 12oz) sweet potato leaves, washed and finely chopped

4–6 scotch bonnet chillies (seeds left in), ½ ground to a paste in a pestle and mortar, ½ left whole, or to taste

plain boiled rice, to serve

Grind the ogirie and the 2 tsp salt in a pestle and mortar, then transfer to a large saucepan or stockpot. Add the goat meat, stock, palm oil and aubergine, if using. Bring to a boil over medium heat, then turn down the heat and simmer, stirring occasionally, until the meat is tender and soft but not falling apart. This process might take up to 60 minutes.

Meanwhile, if you are using anchovies, soak them for about 30 minutes and rinse a couple of times with fresh clean water to get rid of the salt. Set aside. If you are using dried smoked fish, rinse and set aside. Halve the jakato and set aside.

Add the prepared anchovies or dried fish to the pan with the onions, drained butter beans and jakato. Cook until the liquid is reduced by a third. You want to make sure there is very little liquid in the pan, as the sweet potato leaves just need to be steamed for a short time; we still want to see the greens and not overcook the leaves.

When it's ready, add the sweet potato leaves and chillies and cook, stirring, for 10–15 minutes. Taste and add more salt if needed. Allow it to rest for about 10 minutes then serve with plain boiled rice.

CASSAVA LEAF SAUCE/CASSADA LIF PLASAS/SAKI

When people think of Sierra Leone and our abundant resources, they tend to think of diamonds or minerals – but this is our true national treasure. We have many different types of plasas (leafy green sauces), and this is the one and only, the Salone C-Bomb.

If you go to a Sierra Leonean's house, they will usually offer you food. That's our culture. If they offer you our national treasure, our beloved cassava leaf plasas, then they are offering their heart. The absolutely gorgeous smell of perfectly cooked cassada lif in coconut oil is beyond compare. My words cannot do it justice.

100g (3½ oz) ogirie (fermented sesame seeds)

4 tsp salt or to taste

2kg (4lb 8oz) goat meat on the bone, diced (you might be able to buy this frozen in 1kg/2lb 4oz bags in African shops)

700g (1lb 9oz) packet ground cassava leaves

1.5 litres (52fl oz/6½ cups) beef stock

350g (12oz) natural sugar-free smooth peanut butter (use one without palm oil)

500g (1lb 2oz) dried smoked fish fillets, such as barracuda or snapper, available from African shops (see note on page 245)

400g (14oz) can butter beans, drained

400g (14oz) onions (about 2 medium), finely chopped

500ml (17fl oz/2 cups plus 2 tbsp) coconut oil

6 scotch bonnet chillies, seeds left in, to taste, ground to a paste in a pestle and mortar

3–4 tsp dried okra powder

plain boiled rice, to serve

Grind the ogirie in a pestle and mortar with 1 tsp of the salt.

Put the goat meat, ground ogiri, cassava leaves and stock in large stock pot. Bring to the boil, then reduce to a simmer, cover with the lid and simmer for 30–40 mins or until the meat is soft and tender.

Rinse the dried smoked fish fillets. Add the peanut butter and dried smoked fish to the pot, stir well and cook on medium-low heat for about 20 minutes. The sauce will be thick and will start to spatter when you stir, so be careful.

Add the drained butter beans, onions, coconut oil, chillies and 2 tsp of the salt. Stir to incorporate and cook for a further 20–30 or until sauce the sauce is thick.

Add the dried okra powder to the sauce, 1 teaspoon at a time, making sure to watch out for the spatters. Continue adding dried okra powder and stirring in until the sauce has a thick consistency.

Cover the pot and cook for a further 5–10 minutes, then turn off the heat and leave for 10 minutes. Taste, adding more salt if needed, and serve with plain boiled rice.

SWEET POTATO LEAVES AND OKRA SAUCE

I find that cooking is relaxing and makes me feel at home wherever I am. It reminds me of home and, as they say, home is where the heart is. I love living in the UK. My husband and children are here, and I've been here for a while now, so it actually feels like home.

However, Freetown will always be home to me, too, and I'm sure I'm not alone when I say that I have that undeniable feeling that our feet may leave, but not our hearts.

Popeye was right about spinach. Dark green, leafy vegetables are the healthiest foods on the planet. Shame he didn't know about sweet potato leaves and the other dark green vegetables consumed in Sierra Leone.

75g (2¹/₂oz) ogirie (fermented sesame seeds)

2 tsp salt, plus extra to taste

1kg (2lb 4oz) goat meat on the bone, diced (you might be able to buy this frozen in 1kg/2lb 4oz bags in African shops)

1 litre (35fl oz/4 ¹/₃ cups) beef stock

300ml (10¹/₂fl oz/1¹/₄ cups) red palm oil

400g (14oz) smoked barracuda or smoked snapper fillets, rinsed, skin and bones removed, flesh flaked

250g (9oz) onions (about 1 large), finely chopped

8 large jakato (garden eggs), halved if large

250g (9oz) fresh okra, finely chopped

4–6 scotch bonnet chillies (seeds left in), or to taste, ground to a paste in a pestle and mortar

500g (1lb 2oz) sweet potato leaves, chopped

plain boiled rice, to serve

Grind the ogirie with the 2 tsp salt in a pestle and mortar then transfer to a large saucepan or stockpot. Add the goat meat, stock and palm oil to the pan, bring to a boil over medium heat, then turn down the heat and simmer, stirring occasionally, until the meat is tender and soft; this will take up to 60 minutes.

Add the smoked barracuda to the pan with onions and jakato. Cook, stirring occasionally, until the liquid is reduced by half (this will take about 30 minutes). You want to make sure there is not too much liquid in the pan, as the last ingredient, the sweet potato leaves, just need to be steamed for a short time; we still want to see the greens and not overcook the leaves.

Add the okra and chillies to pan and cook for about 10–15 minutes. Add the sweet potato leaves, stir, taste and add more salt if needed. Cook for 5–10 minutes, turn off the heat and leave rest for about 10 minutes. Serve with plain boiled rice.

OKRA STEW

In Sierra Leone, okra stew is served with rice, while okra soup (cooked with palm oil, see page 144) or white okra (no oil) is served with rice or fufu. Most Sundays we eat some kind of stew; okra stew was always one that I looked forward to. The secret is in the texture of rice you serve with it.

Okra is of uncertain parentage. Its geographical origin is disputed, with supporters of South Asian, Ethiopian and West African origins. The Egyptians and Moors of the 12th and 13th centuries used the Arabic word for the plant, *bamya*, suggesting it had come into Egypt from Arabia, but earlier it was probably taken from Ethiopia to Arabia.

In West Africa we have eaten okra for centuries and, because of the transatlantic slave trade, familiar dishes are cooked in the Caribbean and the southern states of the USA.

4 mackerel, heads removed, scaled and gutted (save the heads to make fish stock for another dish)

50g (1¾oz) premium dried anchovies, available from African or Asian shops

100ml (3½fl oz/7 tbsp) sunflower oil, plus 3 tbsp for frying fish

300g (10½ oz) onions (about 1½ medium), finely chopped

2–3 tsp Salone Fire Chilli Sauce (or chilli sauce of your choice), or to taste

½ tsp West African Pepper Blend (see page 23)

500g (1lb 2oz) fresh okra, finely chopped

1 fish or chicken stock pot (I use Knorr)

salt

plain boiled rice, to serve

Wash the mackerel, pat them dry, cut each fish into 3 even chunks and season with salt. Soak the dried anchovies for 30 minutes and rinse a couple of times with fresh clean water to get rid of salt. Set aside.

Heat the 3 tablespoons of oil in a non-stick frying pan on medium heat. When hot, add the mackerel in batches, frying for 3–4 minutes on each side. Using a slotted spoon, transfer the cooked fish to a plate while you cook the remaining batches. Set aside.

In a large saucepan or stockpot, heat the 100ml (3½fl oz/7 tbsp) sunflower oil then add the onions. Cook gently over medium heat, stirring occasionally, until the onions are caramelized and sweet. This process can take up to 45 minutes and mustn't be rushed.

Add the anchovies, the Salone Fire Chilli Sauce and the West African Pepper Blend. Stir and cook for 5 minutes. Add the okra, stir, cover with the lid and cook for 5 minutes.

Add the stock pot, the fried mackerel and a splash of water if needed to prevent the stew from sticking on the base of the pan.

Cook for about 15 minutes, stirring carefully so as not to break up the fish. Taste and season, turn off heat and rest for 10 minutes. Serve with plain boiled rice.

OKRA SOUP

There is a great deal of ceremony that goes into cooking traditional Sierra Leonean dishes and teaching you how to use your senses is the number-one lesson. The right smell to the ogirie as it cooks, the right type of fish, the best palm oil and also the right type of rice to serve it with. These are all things that get passed down from one generation to the other. It's incredibly important that we preserve these skills, otherwise they will be lost forever. I learned to cook traditional Sierra Leonean dishes from my mother and my grandmother, and I do worry my generation will be one of the last with this knowledge.

I think mackerel is a beautiful fish. Its distinctive coat of shimmering silver and green is stunning to look as. It's also packed with goodness and is a tasty way of getting good healthy fish oils into your body. I really like it with okra.

100g (3½ oz) dried smoked fish, available from African and Asian shops (see note on page 245), or dried anchovies

80g (2¾oz) ogirie (fermented sesame seeds)

2 tsp salt, plus extra

1kg (2lb 4oz) goat meat on the bone, diced (you might be able to buy this frozen in 1kg/2lb 4oz bags in African shops)

1.5 litres (52fl oz/6½ cups) beef stock

300ml (10½fl oz/1¼ cups) red palm oil

6 whole mackerel, cleaned and gutted

700g (1lb 9oz) fresh okra, finely chopped

400g (14oz) onions (about 2 medium), finely chopped

6 scotch bonnet chillies (seeds left in), or to taste, ground to a paste in a pestle and mortar

plain boiled rice, fufu or Garri Eba (see page160), to serve

If you are using anchovies, soak them for about 30 minutes and rinse a couple of times with fresh clean water to get rid of the salt. Set aside. If you are using dried smoked fish, rinse and set aside.

Grind the ogirie with the 2 tsp salt in a pestle and mortar then transfer to a large saucepan or stockpot. Add the goat meat, stock and palm oil, bring to a boil over medium heat, then turn down the heat and simmer, stirring occasionally, until the meat is tender and soft; this will take up to 60 minutes.

Cut the heads off the mackerel and save to make fish stock for another dish. Cut each mackerel into 3 even chunks, season with salt and set aside.

Add the anchovies or dried fish to the pan and cook until the liquid is reduced by half, about 30 minutes.

Add the okra, onions and chillies to the pan, cook for 10–15 minutes, then add the mackerel chunks. Cook for a further 10 minutes, stirring very gently to avoid breaking up the fish. Taste and add more salt if needed. Turn off the heat and leave rest for about 10 minutes, then serve with plain boiled rice, fufu or Garri Eba (see page 160).

KRAIN KRAIN (JUTE LEAVES)

This is one of our greens that we cook with a lot. Krain krain (aka jute leaves) are destemmed, cut finely and cooked in a base sauce. Its texture is intentionally, and pleasantly, slimy. The leaves, when harvested young, are generally flavourful and tender; older leaves tend to be fibrous and woody. They are very similar in consistency when cooked to okra.

Jute leaves are not just for culinary uses but are also known for their medicinal properties and are used to make rope, paper and a variety of other products. When cooked as they are here you can serve them with rice – or you can make them extra slimy by using your hands to mix the leaves with the bicarbonate of soda (baking soda), which is recommended if you're serving it with fufu. The bicarbonate of soda also helps preserve the green colour.

100g (3½ oz) dried smoked fish, available from African and Asian shops (see note on page 245), or dried anchovies

1kg (2lb 4oz) or 4 large bundles jute leaves

100g (3½ oz) ogirie (fermented sesame seeds)

2 tsp salt, plus extra to taste

1.5kg (3lb 5oz) goat meat on the bone, diced (you might be able to buy this frozen in 1kg/2lb 4oz bags in African shops)

1 litre (35fl oz/4⅓ cups) beef stock

300ml (10½fl oz/1¼ cups) red palm oil

¼ tsp bicarbonate of soda (baking soda), optional

400g (14oz) onions (about 2 medium), finely chopped

6 scotch bonnet chillies (seeds left in) or to taste, ground to a paste in a pestle and mortar

plain boiled rice or fufu, to serve

If you are using anchovies, soak them for about 30 minutes and rinse a couple of times with fresh clean water to get rid of the salt. Set aside. If you are using dried smoked fish, rinse and set aside.

Pick the jute leaves from the stems (discard the stems), wash the leaves and finely chop. (You can buy ready-prepared jute leaves at African and Asian shops.) Set aside in a bowl until ready to use.

Grind the ogirie and 2 teaspoons salt in a pestle and mortar then transfer to a large saucepan or stock pot. Add the goat meat, stock, ground ogirie and palm oil. Bring to the boil over medium heat, then turn down the heat and simmer, stirring occasionally, until the meat is tender and soft; this will take up to 60 minutes.

Add the anchovies or dried fish to the pan with the onions and chillies. Cook, stirring occasionally, until the liquid is reduced by one third, about 30 minutes.

Sprinkle the bicarbonate of soda (baking soda), if using, over the jute leaves and mix in well. Add the jute leaves to the pan and simmer, stirring occasionally, for 15–20 minutes. Taste and season, adding more salt if needed. Leave to rest for 10 minutes then serve with plain boiled rice or fufu.

VISITING MY GRANDMOTHER

On our trip to Sierra Leone for this book, we visited a market in Bo (the second largest city) for ingredients before travelling to Bandajuma, where my great-grandmother had lived. Bo market was just as I had remembered; very loud and crowded. I felt as if I was in my element! I never really needed to use my tribal language, Mende, when I lived in Freetown because most people spoke Krio; it was just something I knew. Living in England I had even less reason to use it and it had grown rusty, so maybe it was the setting as in the market it all came back, which was a very bizarre but interesting experience.

The drive to Bandajuma was very rough. It wasn't as crowed but the road was underdeveloped, which led to a bumpy ride. It's safe to say that when we arrived in Bandajuma the welcome was more than warm and, sitting here now, I still do not know how I did not cry that day. They had closed the primary school to welcome us and as we pulled up, all the children ran up to the car chanting 'Welcome home!' But the real tear-jerking moment was when I was finally reunited with my grandmother. It had been years since we had seen each other, and she was a lot smaller and frailer than I remembered as she stood in the midst of the crowd beaming and grinning from ear to ear. Although I did well in the Bo markets, the Mende in the villages was much deeper and more accented, so I was helped by a translator, Francis. As well as the language, he also had a

better understanding of all the cultural nuances that came with entering a village, which helped us greet the elders and chiefs respectfully.

After that we went into my great-grandmother's house. It was strange, eerie almost, but in a good way, if that's possible. Throughout my time in the village, I felt that my great-grandmother's presence was very much alive. She had been gone for over 20 years, but those who remembered her retold her stories as if they were scriptures from the Bible. The most memorable one was from when I first came to the village as a toddler.

Back then I could only speak Krio, which led to many uncomfortable experiences: for example, in Krio 'Mama, wata' means 'Grandma, I want water', however to Mende ears this sounded like the name of my great-grandmother's neighbour, Mama Wata. I was told she was bitter about this. After all, it was the first time we were meeting, and I seemed to care about her neighbor more than her! My great-grandmother's house was kept in great condition. Over all these years it has been rebuilt by my auntie and taken care of by the caretaker, Mr Tucker. I still faintly remembered the layout of the house and walking through its halls, I was overcome by a wave of nostalgia and sentimentality. A feeling that I was truly lucky to have met my great-grandmother before she died. She was an incredible human being and is still to this day revered and dearly remembered by many.

TOLA SAUCE

The tola tree (*Beilschmiedia mannii*) is native to the rainforests of Sierra Leone. It is a small evergreen tree that can reach up to 10m (33ft) in height. In Sierra Leone, there are many traditional recipes using the flowers, leaves and especially the seeds of this plant. The fruit is a berry with a thin skin that turns red when it reaches maturity, with a seed inside. It blooms in January and bears fruit between October and December. To the local communities, the tola is an important source of income, especially for its wood (commercial names are kanda and kanda rosa), used for the production of window fixtures, furniture, floors, canoes, etc., often as a substitute for mahogany.

The dried seeds and the powder made from them are rich in protein, carbohydrates, calcium and phosphorus. They are used to thicken soups and vegetable dishes. Tola has delicious savoury, earthy tones combined with a nutty, even fruity flavour that it retains even when cooked. Tola nuts and bor-boueh (see page 156) are from two different types of tree and are classified as vegetables in Sierra Leone. In Nigeria, bor-boueh is known as ogbornor. The seeds from both nuts can be dried after harvesting and subsequently ground into powder form.

100g (3½ oz) ogirie (fermented sesame seeds)

1 tsp salt, plus extra to taste

1kg (2lb 4oz) goat meat on the bone, diced (you might be able to buy this frozen in 1kg/2lb 4oz bags in African shops)

1.5 litres (52fl oz/6½ cups) beef stock

200ml (7fl oz/scant 1 cup) red palm oil

25g (1oz) tola powder

400g (14oz) onions (about 2 medium), finely chopped

5 scotch bonnet chillies (seeds left in), ground to a paste in a pestle and mortar

4 smoked mackerel fillets, skin and bones removed, flesh flaked

plain boiled rice, fufu or Garri Eba (see page 160), to serve

Grind the ogirie and 1 teaspoon salt in a pestle and mortar then transfer to a large saucepan or stockpot. Add the goat meat, stock and the palm oil, reserving 2 tablespoons to mix with the tola powder (see below). Bring to a boil over medium heat then simmer, stirring occasionally, until the meat is soft and tender; this will take up to 60 minutes.

When the meat is tender, turn up the heat slightly and cook to reduce the liquid by about half, about 30 minutes.

Mix the tola powder with the reserved 2 tablespoons of palm oil to prevent it from getting lumpy when it is added to the pan. Add the tola to the pan along with the onions and chillies. Cook for 10–15 minutes, stirring, then add the flaked mackerel. Cook for a further 10 minutes, stirring carefully to avoid breaking up the fish.

Taste and season, adding more salt if needed. Turn off the heat and leave rest for about 10 minutes, then serve with plain boiled rice, fufu or Garri Eba (see page 160).

SERVES 6-8

BOR-BOUEH SAUCE

Bor-boueh (known as ogbono in Nigeria) seeds come from the fruit of trees in the Irvingia genus of African and South East Asian trees. It is also known by the common names wild mango, African mango, bush mango, dika or mbukpap uyo. The edible mango-like fruits and are especially valued for their fat- and protein-rich seeds and are used to thicken soups and stews.

In Sierra Leone each tribe has its own spin on cooking traditional dishes. This dish is predominantly cooked by the Mende people. This sauce gets thicker as it stands, so if you are not planning to serve it immediately, make the sauce slightly lighter.

50g (1¾oz) dried butter beans

30g (1oz) bor-boueh seeds

100g (3½ oz) ogirie (fermented sesame seeds)

1 tsp salt, plus extra to taste

1kg (2lb 4oz) goat meat on the bone, diced (you might be able to buy this frozen in 1kg/2lb 4oz bags in African shops; thaw before using)

1.5 litres (52fl oz/6½ cups) beef stock

150ml (5fl oz/scant ⅔ cup) red palm oil

400g (14oz) onions (about 2 medium), finely chopped

5 scotch bonnet chillies (seeds left in), ground into paste in a pestle and mortar

4 smoked mackerel fillets, skin, bones removed, and flesh flaked

plain boiled rice, fufu or (see page 160), to serve

Lightly toast the dried butter beans in a dry frying pan, then grind them to a powder in a pestle and mortar or blender. Pass the powder through a fine sieve (strainer) and set aside.

Grind the bor-boueh seeds in a pestle and mortar until smooth, form into a ball and set aside.

Grind the ogirie and 1 teaspoon salt in a pestle and mortar then transfer to a large saucepan or stockpot. Add the goat meat, stock and palm oil to the pan and bring to the boil over medium heat. Turn down the heat and simmer, stirring occasionally, until the meat is soft and tender but not falling apart, about 60 minutes. (If you're using frozen meat, this will already be slightly more tender, so may need less cooking time.)

Add the powdered butter beans powder and cook for 10 minutes.

Using a grater, grate the ball of bor-boueh into the sauce. Stir, then add onions and chillies to the pan, cook for 10–15 minutes, stir again, then add the flaked mackerel. Cook for a further 10 minutes, stirring carefully to avoid breaking up the fish.

If the sauce gets too thick, add some water to loosen. Taste and adjust seasoning, adding more salt if needed. Turn off the heat and rest for 10 minutes, then serve with plain boiled rice, fufu or Garri Eba (see page 160).

AWOJOH BEANS (BLACK-EYED BEANS WITH PALM OIL)

This is a traditional dish that is usually served at the 40 days ceremony, which is held 40 days after a loved one passes on, observed mainly by Krio people. A bit of this sauce is put aside for the dead, with no salt or fish added. Other tribes celebrate the passing of a loved one differently. For example, with my family being Muslim, we do not put food aside for the dead or pour libations.

Awojoh, loosely translated, means community feast. It can be to celebrate the life of the deceased or for a baby-naming ceremony. When a child is born in Sierra Leone, there is a naming ceremony seven days after the birth. The child is taken out by an elder in the community and shown around the neighbourhood and the child's name is announced for the first time to everyone and there's a celebration with lots of food and family. In my family, there will be a lamb sacrificed or killed and the meat shared with well-wishers.

300g (10½ oz) dried black-eyed beans

60g (2¼oz) ogirie (fermented sesame paste)

1–2 scotch bonnet chillies (seeds left in), or to taste

100g (3½ oz) premium dried anchovies, available from African and Asian shops

100ml (3½fl oz/7 tbsp) red palm oil

1 litre (35fl oz/4⅓ cups) chicken stock

400g (14oz) red onions (about 2 medium), finely chopped

salt

plain boiled rice or boiled cassava, to serve

Put the dried beans in a bowl, pour over water to cover and leave to soak overnight. The next day, drain the beans, put them in a saucepan, cover with fresh water and cook at a gentle simmer until soft, around 60 minutes. Drain, crush some of the beans using the back of a large metal spoon to help thicken the sauce, and set aside in the sieve (strainer).

Meanwhile, grind the ogirie and chillies to a paste in a pestle and mortar and set aside. Soak the dried anchovies in a bowl of water for 30 minutes, then rinse well to get rid of excess salt.

Put the palm oil, rinsed anchovies, ogirie and chilli paste and the stock in a large saucepan, bring to the boil and cook for about 60 minutes over medium heat with the lid on.

Add the drained beans and the onions to the pan. Bring to a boil, then lower the heat and simmer gently for 30–40 minutes, stirring frequently to make sure nothing sticks to the base of the pan.

At the end of cooking, the liquid should have reduced to a thick, well-flavoured sauce. Taste and season as needed.

Simmer for about 5 more minutes then turn off the heat. Serve warm with plain boiled rice or boiled cassava.

PEMAHUN

Pemahun means 'put it on top' in Mende. This is a very popular all-day breakfast with Mende people. It's super healthy and is recommended to pregnant women and nursing mothers. Growing up, I had two favourite breakfasts, and this was one of them.

This is our very own 'wallah res' (wallah rice), which is chunky with a very nice texture (you can find it in African food shops, such as Khadie Fresh in London). Wallah is a chiefdom in Kambia district in the Northern Province of Sierra Leone, where there is fertile soil for rice cultivation. Kambia District is home to the largest population of ethnic Susu in Sierra Leone. My father is ethnic Susu, but his family settled in Southern Province when they arrived in Sierra Leone from Guinea.

Rice cultivation in West Africa has an extensive and rich history, dating back to around 3,500 years ago, when Africans living in the tropical regions began growing rice in this part of Africa. At the height of the Atlantic slave trade, members from several ethnic groups in and around Sierra Leone were captured, transported, and sold into slavery because of their knowledge of rice cultivation. Many of them were shipped directly to the coastal regions of South Carolina and Georgia in the US.

50g (1¾oz) dried smoked fish, available from African and Asian shops (see page 245), or dried anchovies

420g (15oz) wallah rice or brown rice

800ml–1 litre (28fl oz– 35fl oz/ 3¾ cups–4 ⅓ cups) vegetable stock

6 jakato (garden eggs), tops cut off

40g (1½oz) ogirie (fermented sesame seeds)

4 scotch bonnet chillies (seeds left in), or to taste

500g (1lb 2oz) sweet potato leaves, washed and chopped

2–3 tbsp red palm oil (optional)

salt

If you are using anchovies, soak them for about 30 minutes and rinse a couple of times with fresh clean water to get rid of the salt. Set aside. If you are using dried smoked fish, rinse and set aside.

Put the rice in a sieve (strainer) and rinse under cold water for 10–15 seconds, swirling it around to get rid of excess starch. Transfer the rice to a large saucepan (use one with a lid) and add 800ml (28fl oz) of the vegetable stock. Cover with the lid, turn the heat to medium-high and bring to a boil.

When the rice just starts to boil, reduce the heat so it maintains a gentle simmer and keep the lid on. Add the jakato and continue to cook for about 30 minutes.

While the rice is cooking, grind the anchovies or smoked fish, ogirie and chillies in a food processer to form a paste. Set aside. After 25 minutes, check the rice; there shouldn't be any excess liquid in the pan and the texture of the rice should be al dente. (If the rice needs more liquid, add a bit of the remaining vegetable stock.)

Add the prepared sweet potato leaves to the pan, on top of the rice, followed by the fish, ogirie and chilli paste, putting the paste on top of the sweet potato leaves (don't mix it in). Cover and cook for 10–15 minutes then turn off the heat.

Remove the sweet potato leaves and the flavouring paste from the pan and mix them together in a bowl. Remove the jakato, crush with a fork and add to the bowl with the sweet potato leaves. Add the palm oil, if using, season to taste with salt and keep warm. (Keep the lid on the rice so it can continue to steam in the residual heat.)

Serve the sweet potato leaves sauce on top of the rice.

GARRI EBA

Eba is made with dried, toasted, granulated cassava called garri, which you can buy ready-made or make yourself (not to be confused with cassava flour). Fufu is made from fermented cassava. The tart and sour flavour of starches like these pairs really well with full-bodied and well-seasoned meat and vegetable dishes.

450ml (16fl oz/2 cups) water

450g (1lb) garri (dried, toasted, granulated cassava)

Bring the measured water to the boil in a medium saucepan.

Add the garri and stir vigorously using a wooden spatula until it is smooth, lump-free and cooked through, 15–20 minutes. You will know the eba is cooked through when it is no longer white; the final result will be off-white in colour. Form into dough balls and serve.

BITTER LEAF AND BOLOGIE (SPINACH)

Sierra Leoneans, and West Africans generally, use a variety of leaves in cooking. Here is a dish that uses bologie (spinach) and bittas. The botanical name for bittas is *Vernonia amygdalina*. It is a leafy shrub or small tree that grows in tropical Africa that can reach up to 6m (20ft) when fully grown. (Fun fact: it's actually a member of the daisy family!) True to its name, bittas is very bitter. You have to wash it thoroughly by rubbing the leaves together under running water until most of the bitterness is gone before cooking with it.

1kg (2lb 4oz) oxtail, chopped

1.5 litres (52fl oz/6½ cups) beef stock

100g (3½oz) ogirie (fermented sesame seeds)

2 tsp salt (or to taste)

1kg (2lb 4oz) goat meat on the bone, diced (you might be able to buy this frozen in 1kg / 2lb 4oz bags in African shops)

300ml (10½fl oz/1¼ cups) red palm oil

150g (5½oz) egusi

50g (9oz) processed frozen bitter leaves (bittas), defrosted

500g (1lb 2oz) smoked barracuda flakes, rinsed

300g (10½oz) onions (about 1½ medium), finely chopped

4 scotch bonnet chillies (seeds left in), or to taste, ground to a paste in a pestle and mortar

500g (1lb 2oz) baby spinach, roughly chopped

Fufu or Garri Eba (see page 160), to serve

Simmer the oxtail and stock in a large saucepan or stockpot over a medium heat for 1 hour. Grind the ogirie and 2 teaspoons of the salt in a pestle and mortar and add to the pan, along with the goat meat and palm oil. Bring to a boil over medium heat then turn down the heat and simmer, stirring occasionally, until the meat is tender, this will take up to 1 hour.

Toast the egusi in a dry frying pan until lightly coloured, then grind to a powder in a pestle and mortar and set aside.

Put the defrosted bitter leaves in a sieve (strainer) and rinse under cold water until the water runs clear and most of the bitter taste is gone (a slight bitter taste is fine). Set aside until ready to use.

Add the smoked barracuda flakes, ground egusi, onions and chillies to the pan with the meat, stir and cover. Cook for a further 30 minutes on a medium-low heat; the meat should be tender at this stage and the oxtail almost falling off the bone.

Add the bitter leaves and spinach to the pan and stir. Taste and adjust the seasoning, adding salt if needed. Cook for 10–15 minutes on low heat, then turn off the heat and let it sit with the lid on for 10 more minutes.

Serve with fufu or Garri Eba (see opposite).

SHAPKA (EGUSI SOUP)

Egusi (also known as agusi, agushi) is the name for the fat- and protein-rich seeds of certain cucurbitaceous plants (squash, melon, gourd), which are dried and ground, then used as a major ingredient in West African cuisine.

This is another Salone classic, and again this is not something you can prepare on the fly. Preparing this and many traditional dishes takes time and is a labour of love. You may find the ogirie and white sorrel/hibiscus petals are challenging to track down. It is, however, well worth it.

This is a classic Saturday food or a Sunday morning breakfast in Sierra Leone and is one of my husband's favourite Sierra Leonean mains. This and bittas (or bitter leaves, see page 242), Tola Sauce (see page 154), Okra Soup (see page 144), and probably a few more. Okay, he's a convert to Sierra Leonean cuisine. Probably didn't have a choice. He's even got a grading system for converting other people of European heritage: white belt (novice) is peanut soup; then Cassava Leaf Plasas (see page 139) is yellow belt; and this is black belt – Salone food Grand Master. At which point there's no turning back.

1kg (2lb 4oz) oxtail, chopped (your butcher will be able to cut it into smaller pieces for you)

1.5 litres (52fl oz/6½ cups) beef stock

100g (3½oz) ogirie (fermented sesame paste)

2 tsp salt (or to taste)

1.5kg (3lb 5oz) goat meat on the bone, diced (you might be able to buy this frozen in 1kg/2lb 4oz bags in African shops)

300ml (10½fl oz/1¼ cups) red palm oil

150g (5½oz) egusi/melon seeds

400g (14oz) pack steamed white sorrel/hibiscus petals, rinsed

300g (10½ oz) smoked barracuda fillets

300g (10½ oz) onions (about 1½ medium), finely chopped

4 scotch bonnet chillies, left whole

fufu or Garri Eba (see page 160), to serve

Simmer the oxtail and stock in a large saucepan or stockpot over a medium heat for 1 hour.

Grind the ogirie and 2 teaspoons of salt in a pestle and mortar and add to the pan with the oxtail. Add the goat meat and palm oil. Bring to the boil, then turn down the heat and simmer, stirring occasionally, until the meat is tender; this will take up to 60 minutes.

In a frying pan, toast the egusi until lightly coloured, then grind to a powder in a pestle and mortar and set aside.

Put the white sorrel/hibiscus petals in a sieve (strainer) and rinse under cold water until most of the sour taste is gone (taste it: a slight sour taste is fine). Squeeze them dry, then blend in a food processer until smooth and set aside.

Rinse the smoked barracuda flakes and add to the pan along with the egusi powder, onions and chillies. Stir and cover with the lid. Cook for a further

30 minutes on a medium-low heat. The meat should be very tender at this stage and the oxtail almost falling off the bone.

Add the blended hibiscus petals to the pan, stir, taste and adjust the seasoning, adding salt if it's needed. Cook for 10 more minutes on low heat, then turn off heat and let the soup sit with the lid on for 10 more minutes.

Serve the soup with fufu or Garri Eba (see page 160).

BLACK-EYED BEAN STEW WITH SEA BREAM

Black-eyed beans, known as binch, are a staple in Sierra Leone, and unlike other traditional Sierra Leonean classics such as plasas or the nutty stews, this dish is all about beans. It is often served with boiled cassava, plain boiled rice or yams. These beans are especially popular for breakfast. It's spicy, it's hearty and nutritious.

Soak the beans the night before you want to make this dish. The flavour of beans that you soak yourself will always have more flavour than canned.

300g (10½ oz) dried black-eyed beans

10g (¼oz) garlic (about 2½ medium cloves)

10g (¼oz) fresh ginger, peeled

1–2 scotch bonnet chillies (seeds left in), or to taste

50g (1¾oz) premium dried anchovies, available from African and Asian shops

5 tbsp sunflower oil, plus 2 tbsp to pan-fry the fish

400g (14oz) onions (about 2 medium), finely chopped

1 tsp cumin seeds, toasted in a dry pan and ground in a pestle and mortar

1 tsp coriander seeds, toasted in a dry pan and ground in a pestle and mortar

1 tsp allspice berries, toasted in a dry pan and ground in a pestle and mortar

200g (7oz) fresh tomatoes, chopped

50g (1¾oz) sugar free, no-salt smooth peanut butter (use one made without palm oil)

800ml (28fl oz/3½ cups) chicken stock

1 bay leaf

½ tsp chopped thyme leaves

6 sea bream fillets

salt

Put the dried beans in a bowl, pour over water to cover and leave to soak overnight. The next day, drain the beans, put them in a saucepan, cover with fresh water and cook at a gentle simmer until soft, skimming off the scum from time to time, for 30–40 minutes. Drain and set aside in the sieve (strainer).

Meanwhile, grind the garlic, ginger and chillies to a paste in a pestle and mortar or food processor and set aside.

Soak the dried anchovies in a bowl of water for 30 minutes, then rinse well to get rid of excess salt.

In a large saucepan, heat the 5 tablespoons of oil, add the onions and cook gently, stirring, until soft, 10–15 minutes. Add the ginger, garlic and chilli paste and the anchovies and cook, stirring, for 1 minute. Add the spices and cook for another minute, stirring to thoroughly combine.

Add the drained beans, tomatoes, peanut butter, stock and herbs to the pan. Bring to the boil, then lower the heat and simmer gently for about 1 hour, stirring frequently to make sure nothing is sticking to the base of the pan. At the end of cooking, the liquid should have reduced to a well-flavoured sauce. Remove and discard the bay leaf.

Heat the remaining oil in a large non-stick frying pan on medium-high heat. Season the bream fillets with salt. When the oil is hot, carefully lay in the fish, skin-side down, and cook for 3 minutes. Use a spatula to press the fish gently into the pan for the first 30 seconds of cooking to stop it curling up but don't move it or the skin won't be crispy! Turn the fish over and cook for 2 minutes more.

When the fish are cooked, add them to the pan, on top of the beans (you may need to cut the fish in half to fit everything in the pan). Be very careful not to break up the fillets. Simmer for 5 more minutes, then turn off the heat and serve.

FISH BALL STEW

I'm frequently fascinated by how resourceful we Sierra Leoneans are. When I was a child, I loved eating fish balls. Cooking fish balls was actually part of my mother's strategy to make ends meet. Women in Sierra Leone are very resourceful, and when things are tight and a household is under stress, they employ certain strategies to mitigate the situation. This may be the consumption of less-expensive ingredients and dishes. My mother's fish balls made a little go a long way, using inexpensive fish, onions, herbs, peanut butter and spices.

Coping strategies like this are often employed by families in Sierra Leone. The memories and techniques have stayed with me, and I have re-created my mum's dish here.

FOR THE FISH BALLS

500g (1lb 2oz) haddock fillet or any firm white fish, cut into chunks

2 garlic cloves, chopped

1 small onion, chopped

1 scotch bonnet chilli, chopped

½ thumb-sized piece fresh ginger, peeled and chopped

4 tsp sugar free, no-salt smooth peanut butter (use one made without palm oil)

1 fish or chicken stock cube (use one without MSG), crumbled

oil, for deep frying

salt

FOR THE STEW

120ml (4fl oz/½ cup) cold-pressed coconut oil

500g (1lb 2oz) onions (about 2 large), finely chopped

2–3 tsp Salone Fire Chilli Sauce (or chilli sauce of your choice), or to taste

200g (7oz) fresh tomatoes, chopped

1–2 tsp tomato purée (paste)

1 thyme sprig

1 bay leaf

Checked Rice (see page 175), Coconut Rice (see page 114), boiled cassava or fonio, to serve

For the fish balls, put all the ingredients, except the oil, in a food processor and pulse until the mixture is finely minced.

Take a walnut-size piece of the mixture and form it into a ball. Using a slotted spoon, drop it carefully into the hot oil and cook until golden brown. Remove using a slotted spoon, leave to cool, then taste for seasoning. Add salt as needed to the fish ball mixture and mix well. Using a teaspoon, form the mixture into walnut-size balls. Put the balls on a tray ready to fry.

Heat the oil in a large, deep, heavy-based pan no more than half full. Test it's hot enough by dropping a piece of onion into the oil. If it sizzles, rises to the surface and browns in 30–40 seconds, then the oil is ready.

Carefully fry the balls in batches, ensuring each batch is cooked through and brown (cut one open from each batch to test). Remove from the oil using a slotted spoon and set aside.

For the stew, heat the coconut oil in a clean pan over medium heat. Add the onions and cover with a crumpled piece if damp baking paper, ensuring it sits right on the surface of the onions. Cook over gentle heat, checking from time to time, until the onions are well softened and turning golden brown. This process can take up to 1 hour and cannot be rushed as it is the gentle cooking of the onions and the caramelization that gives this stew its rich and slightly sweet taste.

When the onions are cooked, add the Salone Fire Chilli Sauce, chopped tomatoes, tomato purée (paste), thyme and bay leaf. Cook, stirring, for 1–2 minutes then add the fried fish balls. It's very important that no liquid is added to the stew.

Stir and simmer for about 5 minutes, then taste the sauce and season as needed. Serve with Checked Rice (see page 175), Coconut Rice (see page 114), boiled cassava or fonio.

TANGA JESSEI

The name of this dish means shredded cassava in the Mende language. It's popular with Mende people in Sierra Leone, while fufu and eba are Krio dishes. Cassava is an important source of dietary carbohydrates in the tropical and subtropical areas of the world, with its roots providing food for more than 500 million people.

The cassava (also known as manioc) plant has its origin in South America and the tuber has a hard and starchy white flesh. Amazonian Indians used cassava instead of or in addition to rice, potatoes and maize.

Portuguese explorers introduced cassava to Africa through their trade with the coastal communities and nearby islands. Africans then further diffused cassava, and it is now found in almost all parts of tropical Africa. Local people adopted it for several reasons: the cassava plant can be cultivated in shifting systems and it gives a flexible harvest. It is also resistant to locust attacks and drought.

Note: Cassava should not be eaten raw in large quantities because it contains a naturally occurring cyanide that is toxic to humans, and which needs to be eliminated during its preparation. This is done by cooking or fermenting the vegetable.

> 1kg (2lb 4oz) cassava
>
> 1 tsp salt

Peel the cassava then, using a mandoline, shred the cassava into thin, even strips using the julienne attachment.

Transfer the cassava to a large pan, pour over water to cover, add the salt and bring to the boil. Cook for 5–10 minutes until just cooked (it will be tender when tested with a knife).

Drain the cassava in a colander and run cold water over it. Form the cassava shreds into tennis ball-sized pieces and serve with soups or stews – it's perfect with pepe soup as a main dish.

PALM OIL STEW WITH SNAPPER

Whenever Granny Mariama use to come to stay, she'd give us a teaspoon of palm oil every morning, saying it would help improve our eyesight. My grandmother – nobody knows her age – is one of the fittest old ladies I know. Not saying it's just palm oil, but it has made me more inquisitive about our foods and their nutritional values. Palm oil can also be used to preserve smoked fish; the possibilities of West African palm oil are endless.

20g (³/₄oz) fresh ginger

15g (¹/₂oz) garlic (about 6 cloves)

2–4 scotch bonnet chillies (seeds left in), to taste

1 aubergine (about 350g/12oz)

100ml (3¹/₂fl oz/7 tbsp) red palm oil, plus 3 tbsp to pan-fry the fish

2 large red onions, finely chopped

5g (1 tsp) West African Pepper Blend (see page 23), optional

200g (7oz) fresh tomatoes, chopped

50g (1³/₄oz) tomato purée (paste)

50g (1³/₄oz) dried smoked fish, available from African and Asian shops (see note on page 245), or dried anchovies

1.5 litres (52fl oz/6¹/₂ cups) chicken stock

6–8 jakato (garden eggs)

6 snapper fillets

fresh basil leaves (patmenji in Sierra Leone)

salt

Checked Rice (see page 175), to serve

Blend the ginger, garlic and chillies to a paste in a food processor and set aside.

Peel and finely slice the aubergine and put the slices a large bowl of water to prevent discoloration.

Meanwhile, if you are using anchovies, soak them for about 30 minutes and rinse a couple of times with fresh clean water to get rid of the salt. Set aside. If you are using dried smoked fish, rinse and set aside.

Heat the palm oil in a large heavy-based pan with lid. Add the onions, reduce the heat, and cook gently, stirring from time to time until they are soft, 10–15 minutes.

Add the ginger, garlic and chilli paste and cook, stirring, for 2–3 minutes, turning the heat down if it starts to stick on the base of the pan. Add the aubergine slices and cook, stirring occasionally, until soft, 10–15 minutes. Add a splash of stock if it starts to stick.

Add the West African Pepper Blend (if using) and cook for a further 1 minute, then add the chopped tomatoes, tomato purée (paste) and the anchovies or dried fish. Cook for 3–5 minutes to get all the flavours to marry together.

Add the stock and the jakato and cook on low-medium heat until the sauce is reduced by half, about 30 minutes.

While the sauce is reducing, pan-fry the snapper. Heat the 3 tablespoons red palm oil in a non-stick frying pan. When hot, add the fillets and cook for 3 minutes on each side or until cooked through (you may need to work in batches). Set aside.

Once the sauce is reduced, taste and adjust seasoning, adding salt if needed. Gently add the fried fish and the basil leaves, being careful to leave the fish as whole as possible. Simmer for 5 minutes and turn off the heat. Allow to sit for a few minutes and serve with Checked Rice (see page 175).

CHECKED RICE (RICE WITH JUTE LEAVES)

Sierra Leonean checked rice is a much-loved rice dish in Freetown and among the diaspora. This rice is made with jute leaves which, when cooked, have the same texture that okra imparts to a dish. Jute leaf is an edible leaf from certain types of jute plants and is often used to thicken soups, stews and sauces.

500g (1lb 2oz) basmati rice

750ml (26fl oz/3¼ cups) water

1 tsp salt

300g (10½ oz) prepared jute leaves (frozen leaves work well here; defrost if frozen)

pinch of bicarbonate of soda (baking soda)

Put the rice in a large bowl and add cold water to cover. Using your hands, gently swirl the grains to release the excess starch. Pour away the water and repeat this process a couple of times until the water runs clear. Drain the rice through a fine mesh sieve (strainer).

Bring the measured water and salt to a boil in a large pan (use one with a tight-fitting lid) and add the rice. Give it a stir and cover the pot with the lid, turn heat down to a simmer and cook the rice for 15–20 minutes or until all the water is absorbed.

Meanwhile, mix the jute leaves in a bowl with the bicarbonate soda (baking soda). The bicarbonate helps cook the jute leaves faster and stops the leaves from turning brown once steamed.

When the rice is almost cooked, make a little well in the middle of the rice and add the jute leaves and bicarbonate (baking soda). Put the lid back on and leave to steam for about 5 minutes. Turn off the heat, remove the jute leaves from the pan and transfer to a bowl. Cover to keep warm and set aside.

Allow the rice to sit, off the heat with the lid on, for about 5 minutes, then fluff with a fork and mix in the jute leaves. Serve with Palm Oil Stew with Snapper (see page 170) or any other stew.

SWEET POTATO LEAF STEW

Both the leaves and the tubers of sweet potatoes are eaten in a variety of soups, stews and sauces. They are accessible both in the dry and wet seasons, making them a good substitute for rice. Unlike cassava, practically all sweet potatoes are consumed fresh.

Sweet potato production has expanded in recent years across Sierra Leone. Growing sweet potatoes is attractive to farmers because of the vegetable's adaptability to different environments, and they are an important source of food during the lean season.

100g (3½oz) dried smoked fish, available from African or Asian shops (see note on page 245), or dried anchovies

1 aubergine (optional)

200ml (7fl oz/scant 1 cup) coconut oil, plus 3 tbsp to pan-fry the fish

400g (14oz) onions (about 2 medium), finely chopped

100ml (3½fl oz/7 tbsp) water (you may not need it all)

3 scotch bonnet chillies (seeds left in), left whole

1 chicken stock cube (use one without MSG)

8 large jakato (garden eggs), stems removed, halved

6 snapper fillets

800g (1lb 12oz) sweet potato leaves, washed and finely chopped

salt, to taste

plain boiled ice, to serve

If you are using anchovies, soak them for about 30 minutes and rinse a couple of times with fresh clean water to get rid of the salt. Set aside. If you are using dried smoked fish, rinse and set aside.

Peel and finely slice the aubergine (if using) and put in a bowl with water to cover to prevent browning.

Heat the coconut oil in a pan (use one with a lid) over medium heat. Add the onions and cook over gentle heat, stirring from time to time, until they are well softened and turning golden brown, 10–15 minutes. Add the aubergine, adding a splash of the measured water if it starts to stick on the base of the pan. Cover with the lid and cook until the aubergine is soft, 10–15 minutes.

Add the chillies and anchovies (or dried fish), the stock cube and the jakato. Cook for 10–15 minutes, stirring frequently, adding a splash of the water if it gets too dry and starts to stick to pan.

Meanwhile, heat the 3 tablespoons of coconut oil in a non-stick frying pan and fry the snapper for about 3 minutes on each side (you may need to do this in batches). Set aside.

Add the sweet potato leaves to the stew and cook for about 5–10 minutes, stirring. Taste and adjust the seasoning. Add the fried snapper fillets to the pan and gently incorporate with the sauce, trying not to break up the fillets too much. Cook for another 5 minutes then turn off heat. Leave to rest for about 10 minutes and serve with plain boiled rice.

DESSERTS

RETURNING TO SIERRA LEONE

When we visited my grandmother on our trip to Sierra Leone, the entire community in her village gathered to prepare a meal together. Communal cooking is deeply ingrained in Sierra Leone's culture and since the dawn of time has played huge role in our traditions and ceremonies. For example, in the folk religions of Sierra Leone it is believed that death does not dictate the end of a human life. For a short period after death, the spirit of the deceased lingers and then passes on to another realm from which it 'looks over' the living. Funeral rites are held immediately after death, and a week afterwards the first Awujoh feast is held. This is a big meal, which friends and family cook to offer the dead, in hope that the spirit is appeased and will protect the family from the afterlife. Awujoh feasts can consist of any traditional dish depending on where you live, but the most prevalent components of such feasts are fried sweet potatoes, black-eyed beans and fried plantain.

The biggest Awujoh feast takes place on the 40th day after death, which is recognised as the day the spirit moves on to the afterlife. As the family and guests eat, small portions of the meal are placed in a hole for the dead alongside kola nuts. The last significant event after a death is the first-year anniversary; this day is called *pull na mooning* (meaning 'to come out of mourning'). Traditionally, the bereaved will wear white and visit the cemetery together and then return home for refreshments.

Another ceremony where you might see an Awujoh feast being held is *pull na doh* (meaning 'to take outside'), a birth and naming ceremony brought by the Krio people. It is a social event with a strong sense of spirituality. Traditionally the elders of the community would gather and bestow a name upon the child on the seventh day after their birth. In Sierra Leone, who you are named after is very important. It is believed that there is a connection between the child and the person they were named after. I was named after my grandmother.

Other traditional ceremonies, which are not Krio, include Gbangbanie, which is a coming-of-age ceremony for Limba men, and Kamba for women. Of course, these ceremonies signify the child's coming into adulthood and therefore the question of marriage arises. Whether you are Mende, Loko, Yalunka or Temne, although you might have specific rules and traditions, marriage is celebrated similarly – with lots of food! As part of the engagement, the husband-to-be's family will send a little girl of around 10 years of age, who will be carrying a bottle gourd known as calabash tied with white cloth atop her head. Her young age and the white cloth signify virginity, which is used to embody the purity and sincerity of the groom's intentions.

Inside the calabash will be the bride-dowry, including money in envelopes for specific family members as a sign of respect, a needle and

AFRICAN WEDDINGS NEVER DISAPPOINT. JUST LIKE IN WESTERN CULTURES, THERE WILL FIRST BE A CHURCH OR MOSQUE CEREMONY.

thread, which signifies a willingness to work together as husband and wife, to mend the situation in times of struggle, and kola nuts. In Sierra Leonean culture, kola nuts signify many things. They are used to welcome people, to seal agreements, to mark reconciliations and to show good will. In a marriage, because of their originally bitter taste and sweet finish, they are used to communicate the groom's belief that, as a couple, their love will overcome any obstacles that wait for them in the future.

African weddings never disappoint. Just like in Western cultures, there will first be a church or mosque ceremony (or both, sometimes on the same day – we are a very religion-tolerant nation), after which the couple will go to each of their in-laws' homes to 'drink wata'. At the doorstep of each house, the mother and father will drink from a cup of water, bless the couple, pray on the cup of water, and then pass it to the newlywed couple to drink to complete the ritual and accept the blessings. Finally, there will be a very large event with music, dancing and, of course, a grand feast. This is called ashobi night, as all the guests are expected to wear ashobi, which is a very colourful, decorated uniform fabric seen around all parts of western Africa. From birth to coming of age to marriage, death and transitioning, food sees us through every milestone. In Sierra Leonean culture, food is more than just nourishment; it is what binds us as a community.

On our trip, we were told that we would be climbing the Wara Wara mountains. Apparently, this wouldn't be a difficult hike: it would be around 30 minutes to and fro, and so I was fully convinced that my long dress and trusty pair of trainers would see me through. When we arrived at the village nearby, the chief's wife asked me if I was sure this was the outfit I wanted to wear to go up the mountain. I confidently (and oh-so-naively) told her it was, and a look of concern crossed her face. Instead of 30 minutes back and forth, we took two hours to even get up the mountain and I spent the entire journey huffing and puffing and cursing my life away.

Nevertheless, as we reached the peak all my negative emotions were overcome by pure astonishment. The view from the top of the mountain was beyond exquisite. I mentioned before that the Limba people were the first settlers in Sierra Leone, and it was here, in the Wara Wara mountains, that they found refuge from the conflict and brutality that existed in the outside world. Even during the transatlantic slave trade, the Limba were one of the only tribes that were not taken as slaves. The Wara Wara mountains have protected them for centuries and will continue to do so for centuries more to come.

ROASTED PLANTAIN ICE CREAM

The idea for this dessert came to me one day when I was shopping in East Street Market, in the Walworth district of south east London. There has been street-market trading in the Walworth area since the 16th century and, in the late 1800s, the market officially moved to East Street. These days, south east London is very multicultural and provides an eclectic mix of fresh food, from cassava to courgettes, durian fruit to eel, sheep heads to cow hooves.

On a visit to the market with my dear friend and fellow Salone (Sierra Leonean), Rosaline, we set out to buy plantain. They only had overripe plantain and an idea popped into my head: I realized I could turn these black overripe plantains into ice cream, of the sort that street vendors sell from pushcarts in Freetown. To make the very best plantain ice cream, it's important to use overripe plantain (look for those with black skins).

2 small overripe (black) plantains	5 egg yolks
90g (3¼oz) soft light brown sugar	pinch of salt
15g (½oz/1 tbsp) unsalted butter	1 tsp pure vanilla extract
250ml (9fl oz/generous 1 cup) full-fat (whole) milk	2 tbsp dark rum or brown sugar rum
	hot strong espresso coffee, to serve (optional)
250ml (9fl oz/generous 1 cup) double (heavy) cream	dark chocolate, to serve (optional)

Preheat the oven to 200°C/180°C fan/400°F/gas mark 6.

Peel the plantain, chop them into small chunks and toss in a bowl with the sugar. Transfer to a baking tray, spread out in a single layer and dot over the butter. Bake for 30 minutes or until the plantain is browned and nicely caramelized.

Meanwhile, gently heat the milk and cream in a saucepan over low-medium heat. Bring the mixture up to scalding point then remove from the heat and set aside. Be careful not to let it boil.

Put the egg yolks into a large mixing bowl, whisk briefly, then pour the warm milk and cream mixture onto the yolks. Whisk to combine, then return the mixture to the cleaned-out pan over low-medium heat.

Using a wooden spoon, stir constantly until the mixture thickens to form a custard thick enough to coat the back of the wooden spoon, 5–10 minutes depending on the temperature. Keep the heat low to prevent the mixture from curdling. When it's thickened, remove the pan from the heat and allow to cool.

Scrape the plantain and the thick syrup from the baking tray into a blender then add the custard, salt and vanilla. Blend to a smooth purée.

Chill the mixture thoroughly in the fridge, then transfer to an ice-cream machine, add the rum and churn according to the manufacturer's instructions. Transfer to a freezer-safe plastic container and freeze until needed. **Note:** After chilling, if the mixture is too thick, whisking will thin it out before churning.

Alternatively, you can freeze the puréed mixture in a shallow dish and, when frozen, cut into chunks and blend briefly. Return the portions to the freezer immediately and freeze until needed.

Please remember to take the ice cream out of the freezer and put it the fridge 20–30 minutes before serving to allow it to soften slightly.

Delicious served as an affogato-style dessert drenched in hot espresso coffee with a few squares of dark chocolate melted into it.

TOASTED KOKNAT ICE CREAM

In Sierra Leone, fresh coconut milk and coconut jelly (the flesh of young coconuts) is widely available from street vendors known as 'jelly men' because of the coconut jelly they sell.

The flesh of the mature coconut is usually toasted and we make coconut brittles with it. In this recipe I am using toasted coconut chips to get that toasty flavour of the coconut into the ice cream.

75g (2½oz) toasted coconut chips

100ml (3½fl oz/scant ½ cup) full-fat (whole) milk

300ml (10½fl oz/1¼ cups plus 1 tbsp) double (heavy) cream

200ml (7fl oz/scant 1 cup) coconut milk

6 egg yolks

115g (4oz/½ cup plus 1¼ tbsp) caster (superfine) sugar

½ tbsp vanilla bean paste

pinch of salt

Put the toasted coconut chips in a dry frying pan and warm until fragrant, about 5 minutes, keeping an eye on them so they don't burn.

Pour the milk, cream and coconut milk into a saucepan over medium heat, add the toasted coconut chips and mix to combine. Bring the mixture up to scalding point then remove from the heat and set aside for 1 hour to let the flavours infuse.

Gently rewarm the infused milk and cream mixture. Set a fine-mesh sieve (strainer) over a medium saucepan and strain the coconut-infused liquid through the strainer into the saucepan. Press down on the coconut very firmly using a rubber spatula to extract as much of the flavour as possible. Discard the coconut.

Put the egg yolks into a large mixing bowl with the sugar, vanilla bean paste and salt and mix well. Pour the warm milk and cream mixture onto the yolks. Whisk to combine, then return the mixture to a clean pan over low-medium heat.

Using a wooden spoon, stir constantly until the mixture thickens to form a custard thick enough to coat the back of the wooden spoon, 5–10 minutes depending on the temperature. Keep the heat low to prevent the mixture from curdling. When it's thickened, strain the toasted coconut custard into a bowl and leave to cool completely.

When cool, churn the mixture in an ice-cream machine according to the manufacturer's instructions, then transfer to a freezer-safe plastic container. Freeze until needed.

Please remember to take the ice cream out of the freezer and put it the fridge about 30 minutes before serving to allow it to soften slightly.

SERVES 6

YAM PANCAKES
WITH HIBISCUS BUTTER

My cooking is inspired by my Sierra Leonean heritage, but Afro-fusion cooking
can be traced back to the transatlantic slave trade. Freetown's unique history
has been influenced by Portuguese slave traders, returning Afro-Caribbeans,
Africans and Black people born in the UK and returned to Africa following
the abolition of slavery. Then our city was raided and plundered by French
fleets during the Napoleonic Wars and French revolutionary periods. Lebanese
immigrants came following a silkworm crisis in Lebanon. Then, of course,
there's the British colonial influences.

Afro-fusion cuisine combines elements from other cultures and has actually
influenced our culture and food for centuries. I think the art is to respect
traditional dishes handed down from generation to generation, but let's not
be afraid to elevate this aspect of our culture and draw inspiration from the
many ingredients that are unique to our country and the African continent.

If you have leftover mashed yam, this is a great way to use it up – although
I've also included instructions for beginning with raw yam.

FOR THE YAM PANCAKES

175g (6oz) yam, peeled

2 eggs

1 tsp vanilla extract

200ml (7fl oz/scant 1 cup) full-fat (whole)
  milk, plus extra (optional)

50g (1¾oz/6 tbsp) plain (all-purpose) flour

½ tsp baking powder

2 tbsp sunflower oil

FOR THE HIBISCUS BUTTER

115g (4oz/½ cup) unsalted butter, softened

25g (1oz) hibiscus powder

2 tsp vanilla extract

4 tbsp agave nectar or honey, plus extra
  to drizzle

For the yam pancakes, cut the yam into chunks and cook in boiling water until
tender, about 10 minutes. Drain well and press through a potato ricer (or mash
with a masher). Weigh out 175g (6oz) and set aside to cool (any leftover mashed
yam can be frozen in a freezer-safe plastic container for up to 3 months).

For the hibiscus butter, put all the ingredients in a bowl and whisk until combined,
smooth, light and fluffy.

The hibiscus butter can be made ahead and stored in an airtight container in the
fridge for up to 10 days or in the freezer for 2 months.

Put the mashed yam, eggs, vanilla extract and milk into a blender and blend
until smooth. In a mixing bowl, whisk together the flour and baking powder.
Add the yam mixture and stir until well combined. Add more milk if the batter

is too thick. The batter should be creamy and not too thin, similar to a batter for American-style pancakes.

Heat ½ tablespoon of the sunflower oil in a non-stick frying pan and spoon 2–3 tablespoons of the yam pancake batter into the hot pan. The pancake should be quite thick. Allow to cook for a couple of minutes until the underside is golden brown, then carefully flip over and cook on the other side until golden.

Remove from the pan and keep warm while you cook the remaining batter in the same way, adding more oil to the pan as needed. You should have enough for 4 large pancakes.

Serve the warm pancakes with the hibiscus butter and a drizzle of agave nectar or honey.

MORINGA ICE CREAM

Moringa oleifera is a plant that is often called the drumstick tree, the miracle tree, the ben oil tree or the horseradish tree. Moringa has been used for centuries for its medicinal properties and health benefits. It is also said to have antifungal, antiviral, anti-depressant and anti-inflammatory properties, and contains a variety of proteins, vitamins and minerals.

My mother grows moringa in her compound. She would pick the leaves, dry them and make me tea with them. The flavor of this refreshing treat should be a perfect balance of earthy, sweet and ever-so-slightly bitter.

300ml (10½fl oz/1¼ cups plus 1 tbsp) full-fat (whole) milk

300ml (10½fl oz/1¼ cups plus 1 tbsp) double (heavy) cream

4 tsp dried moringa powder

6 egg yolks

115g (4oz/½ cup plus 1¼ tbsp) caster (superfine) sugar

pinch of salt

Pour the milk and cream into a saucepan over medium heat, add the moringa powder 1 teaspoon at a time and mix until well combined. Bring the mixture up to scalding point then remove from the heat and set aside.

Put the egg yolks into a large mixing bowl with the sugar and salt and mix well. Pour the warm milk and cream mixture onto the yolks. Whisk to combine, then return the mixture to the cleaned-out pan over low-medium heat.

Using a wooden spoon, stir constantly until the mixture thickens to form a custard thick enough to coat the back of the wooden spoon, 5–10 minutes depending on the temperature. Keep the heat low to prevent the mixture from curdling. When it's thickened, strain the moringa custard mixture into a bowl and leave to cool completely.

When cool, churn the mixture in an ice-cream machine according to the manufacturer's instructions, then transfer to a freezer-safe plastic container. Freeze until needed.

Please remember to take the ice cream out of the freezer and put it the fridge about 30 minutes before serving to allow it to soften slightly.

CITRUS FRUIT SALAD

In Sierra Leone we don't really a culture of eating desserts, but it is common for us to eat tropical fruit after dinner.

    2 large oranges
    1 pink grapefruit
    2 tangerines
    ½ small pineapple

On a board set over a lipped tray to catch the juices, peel and segment the oranges, grapefruit and tangerines, taking care to remove all the white pith.

Peel the pineapple, remove the core and cut the flesh into even chunks, about 2cm (¾in), reserving any juice from the fruits.

Mix all the fruits together in a bowl, set aside in the fridge and serve topped with the African Negroni Slushy (see page 197).

MORINGA MOUSSE

Talk about flavoristic. Yeah, boyeeeee! This is what I call Flavor Flav – not a public enemy at all, and when it comes to health benefits, you can't fight the power, but you can believe the hype! In Africa, moringa is used to treat many common ailments but here I've made it into something Shwen Shwen.

African moringa is super-nutritious. Just 100g (3½oz) of fresh moringa leaves provide the same amount of protein as an egg, as much iron as a steak, as much vitamin C as an orange and as much calcium as you would find in a glass of milk. It's a lean, mean super green, jam-packed with nutrition.

Moringa mousse, served with almond biscotti, goes well with a beautiful lightly chilled Vin Santo, a Tuscan dessert wine that lingers on the palate.

You can use the egg yolks, which are not needed for this recipe, to make mayonnaise or aioli.

3 egg whites

100g (3½oz/½ cup) caster (superfine) sugar

1 tbsp dried moringa powder

225ml (7¾fl oz/scant 1 cup) double (heavy) cream

1 tsp vanilla extract

almond biscotti, to serve

Using an electric hand-mixer, whisk the egg whites in a mixing bowl until soft peaks begin to form when the whisk is removed. Add half of the sugar and continue whisking until the mixture stands in stiff peaks. Add the moringa powder and mix gently to incorporate.

Clean the beaters and, in a separate large mixing bowl, whisk the double (heavy) cream just until it begins to thicken up. Add the remaining caster sugar and the vanilla extract and continue gently whisking until the mixture holds a medium peak (when you lift the whisk out of the bowl, the peaks will slightly droop down but it won't lose it shape entirely).

Using a large metal spoon or rubber spatula, fold the cream mixture into the moringa mixture one third at a time until incorporated.

Spoon the mousse into serving glasses, wiping around the sides to tidy them up.

Chill for at least 4 hours before serving with almond biscotti.

AFRICAN NEGRONI SLUSHY

The inspiration for this dessert stems from my Passionately Bissap juice drink, which combines hibiscus petals and Kentish strawberries. The hibiscus brings a tart, almost cranberry-like flavour and a deep red-violet colour, and the strawberries add a succulent sweetness.

In Sierra Leone we use the red hibiscus petals for drinks and the white hibiscus petals for savoury dishes. This recipe combines flavours from my African heritage with the county of Kent where I now live.

40g (1½oz/3¼ tbsp) granulated sugar

125ml (4fl oz/½ cup) water

250ml (9fl oz/generous 1 cup) Shwen Passionately Bissap hibiscus and strawberry juice

125ml (4fl oz/½ cup) Campari

125ml (4fl oz/½ cup) sweet red vermouth

2 tbsp gin

Put the sugar and water in a medium saucepan over medium heat. Bring to the boil, stirring constantly until the sugar dissolves, then increase heat and simmer for 4–5 minutes until the liquid is thick and syrupy. Set aside to cool to room temperature.

Add the rest of the ingredients, stir, then pour the mixture into a freezer-safe container and freeze for 24 hours.

Spoon the slushy over Citrus Fruit Salad (see page 195) arranged in a chilled soup bowl.

STRAWBERRY AND GRAINS OF PARADISE GRANITA

My nickname at my secondary school in Freetown, Albert Academy, was 'Ice'. Not because I was a cool rapper (I was probably the least cool person – I was shy and reserved), but because I spent all my lunch money on ice lollies (ice pops). I never spent my lunch money on substantial food that would fill me up, which meant I was skinny as anything. (Oh, how life's changed; they say Black don't crack, but it does expand.)

By the end of the school day, I was always hungry, so I would end up spending my transport money, which was meant to be for a shared taxi home, on street food and take a slow walk home. Yes, from Circular Road to Cockle Bay Road in Freetown, which was a long walk (it would take me about an hour and half).

So that was me – the original Ice, Ice Baby!

150g (5½oz/¾ cup) granulated sugar

1 tsp roughly ground grains of paradise

600ml (21fl oz/generous 2½ cups) water

400g (14oz) fresh strawberries

juice of 1 lemon

Put the sugar, grains of paradise and measured water in a medium saucepan over medium heat. Bring to the boil, stirring constantly until the sugar dissolves, then increase the heat and simmer for 4–5 minutes until the liquid is thick and syrupy. Set aside to cool.

Blend the strawberries in a blender until smooth, then pass through a sieve (strainer) into a large bowl to remove the seeds (discard the seeds).

Strain the cooled sugar syrup into the strawberry purée, add the lemon juice and stir.

Transfer the mixture to a freezer-safe plastic container and freeze for 1–2 hours. Remove from the freezer and stir with a fork to mix the ice crystals evenly. Return to the freezer and repeat the stirring process 2–3 times every 2 hours until the granita has an even texture of small ice crystals.

Serve the granita in chilled glasses.

BLACK VELVET TAMARIND /BLACK TOMBLAH SORBET

Black velvet tamarind (or black tomblah) is the fruit of the *Dialium guineense* tree, which is indigenous to West Africa. The fruits have a hard, velvety black shell, orange sticky pulp and flat circular brown seeds (the shell and seeds are not eaten). It's very popular with children because it's sweet, although it's time-consuming to peel. It is less sour than tamarind and has a dusty velvet-like feel in your mouth. It's sold dried and already peeled in West African shops in London.

This sorbet takes me down memory lane – the anticipation of carefully peeling a handful of black tomblah and then shoving it all in my mouth at once. It's a flavour explosion.

If you can't find black velvet tamarind, you could substitute sweet tamarind (peel the pods) and adjust the sugar accordingly; you will need more to offset the tart taste.

450g (1lb) peeled, dried black velvet tamarind

500ml (17fl oz/2 cups plus 2 tbsp) hot water

160g (5⅔ oz/¾ cup plus 1 tbsp) caster (superfine) sugar

450ml (16fl oz/2 cups) cold water

juice of 1 lime

1 egg white, beaten until lightly frothy

Put the black velvet tamarind in a heatproof bowl, pour over the measured hot water and leave to soak for 20–30 minutes. When the water is cool enough, use your fingers to squeeze and separate the flesh from the seeds into the water.

Pour the black velvet tamarind mixture (including the water) through a sieve (strainer) set over a bowl to catch the pulp. Use your hands to mix and press the mixture, extracting as much of the pulp possible. Discard the membranes and seeds.

Put the sugar and measured cold water in a medium saucepan over medium heat. Bring to the boil, stirring constantly until the sugar dissolves, then increase heat and simmer for 4–5 minutes until the liquid is thick and syrupy.

Stir the velvet tamarind pulp into the syrup with the lime juice, strain again through a fine sieve (strainer) and leave to cool completely.

When cool, churn the mixture in an ice-cream machine according to the manufacturer's instructions, adding the frothy egg white as the sorbet thickens.

Transfer to a freezer-safe plastic container and freeze for at least 24 hours. Transfer the sorbet to the fridge 20–30 minutes before serving to allow it to soften slightly before serving.

PASSIONATELY BISSAP HIBISCUS AND STRAWBERRY JELLIES

These mini jellies (molded gelatine) absolutely encapsulate summer – they're a celebration of hibiscus. Jelly must be many people's favourite childhood dessert memory. My first-ever connection with Leith's School of Food and Wine in London triggered a conversation about my product range and a suggestion from them that I should consider making jelly with my juices. Here's the recipe.

7 leaves of leaf gelatine or 3½ tsp powdered gelatine

3 tbsp water

600ml (21fl oz/generous 2½ cups) Shwen Passionately Bissap (hibiscus and strawberry juice), or a similar juice mixture of your choice

3–4 tbsp caster (superfine) sugar

If you are using leaf gelatine, soak the gelatine leaves in the measured water (it should be cold) for 4–5 minutes until softened. While they are soaking, place the Passionately Bissap juice (or juices of your choice) in a small pan with the sugar and place over a low heat, stirring occasionally until dissolved.

After the soaking time, squeeze as much liquid as you can from the gelatine and add to the pan. Turn off the heat and stir until the gelatine has also dissolved.

If you are using powdered gelatine, put the measured water into a small saucepan, sprinkle over the powdered gelatine and leave for 5 minutes to allow the gelatine to absorb the water (it will become spongy). Place the pan over the lowest of heat to fully dissolve the gelatine, but please do not stir.

In a second saucepan over low heat, dissolve 3 tablespoons of the sugar in half of the Passionately Bissap juice (or juice of your choice), stirring regularly.

Pour the warm juice mixture into the pan with the melted gelatine and stir well. Stir in the remaining juice. Taste and add the remaining sugar if necessary, then pass through a fine sieve (strainer) into a bowl.

Rinse out 12 x 60ml (2fl oz) mini jelly moulds with cold water then pour in the jelly mixture. Refrigerate for at least 4 hours or until the jellies are completely set.

Take the jellies out of the fridge 30 minutes before serving. To release the jellies from the moulds, loosen the tops with your finger, then give the moulds a sharp side-to-side shake. Turn out onto serving plates and serve with Hibiscus and Greek Yoghurt Ice Cream (see page 204).

HIBISCUS AND GREEK YOGHURT ICE CREAM

This yoghurt ice cream recipe (photograph on page 203) makes a wonderful alternative to a plain old ice cream. The thick Greek yoghurt acts as its base, giving a luxuriously rich and creamy finish without having to make a custard. The Passionately Bissap juice give a nice colour, and it's not overly sweet.

300ml (10½fl oz/1¼ cups plus 1 tbsp) double (heavy) cream

300ml (10½fl oz/1¼ cups plus 1 tbsp) Greek yogurt

360g (13oz/1¾ cups) caster (superfine) sugar

300ml (10½fl oz/1¼ cups plus 1 tbsp) full-fat (whole) milk

3 tbsp hibiscus powder

4 tbsp Shwen Passionately Bissap (hibiscus and strawberry juice)

Whisk the double (heavy) cream in a large mixing bowl until it forms soft peaks when the whisk is removed.

Add the yoghurt, sugar, milk, hibiscus powder and Passionately Bissap juice and whisk gently to combine.

Chill in the fridge for 20 minutes. When cool, transfer the mixture to an ice-cream machine and churn according to the manufacturer's instructions. Transfer to a freezer-safe plastic container and freeze until needed.

Please remember to take the ice cream out of the freezer and put it the fridge about 30 minutes before serving to allow it to soften slightly.

MORINGA GRANITA

The origins of granita date back to the Arab domination of Sicily in the 9th century CE. Arab people brought a recipe of sherbet: a drink made with fruit juice flavoured with rosewater and then iced. Here I use moringa. There's something about eating moringa – you can actually taste the goodness in every mouthful.

600ml (21fl oz/generous 2½ cups) water

2½ tablespoons dried moringa powder

130g (4½ oz/⅔ cup) granulated sugar

Bring the measured water to the boil in a saucepan then lower the heat.

Add the moringa powder and sugar and give it a good whisk until the sugar and moringa powder have dissolved. Leave to cool then pour into a freezer-safe plastic container.

Freeze for 1–2 hours. Remove from the freezer and stir with a fork to mix the ice crystals evenly. Return to the freezer and repeat the stirring process 2–3 times every 2 hours until the granita has an even texture of small ice crystals.

Serve the granita in chilled glasses.

SIERRA LEONEAN-STYLE RICH CAKE

I have fond childhood memories of the preparation process involved in making this cake. We would often cream the butter and sugar by hand using a wooden spoon in Sierra Leone and this could take hours, but the end result was worth it. The next step is where Sierra Leonean ingenuity comes in. We would butter the inside of empty powdered milk tins and use these as baking tins.

The cake was then baked outside in the open on an improvised oven, with a large pot placed on top of three stones, with sand spread across the base. We put the cake tins on top of the hot sand in the pot and put the lid on. Our fuel was wood or charcoal, and when the fuel was very hot, we put lumps of hot charcoal on top of the lid of the pot to brown both the top and bottom of the cake. Experienced outdoor bakers would adjust the heat by spreading out the coals as the cake baked, and wouldn't take the lid off at all as it cooked. How impressive! Try baking outside on an open fire with everyday objects as equipment, and absolutely nailing it. Salone girls rule!

150g (5½ oz/⅔ cup) butter, plus extra for buttering

150g (5½ oz/¾ cup) caster (superfine) sugar

3 eggs

50g (1¾oz/6 tbsp) plain (all-purpose) flour

150g (5¼oz/1 cup plus 2 tbsp) self-raising flour

1–2 tbsp full-fat (whole) milk

finely grated zest of 1 orange

1 tsp natural orange flavouring (I use Steenbergs Organic Orange Extract)

Make sure all the ingredients are at room temperature. Generously butter a 18cm (7in) cake tin. Preheat the oven to 180°C/160°C fan/350°F/gas mark 4.

Using an electric hand-mixer, cream the butter and sugar together in a large mixing bowl until the mixture is pale, light and fluffy (10–15 minutes). Don't rush this step; the more thoroughly the butter and sugar are combined, the lighter the cake will be. Add the eggs, one at a time, beating the mixture well between each addition. Add 1 tablespoon of flour with the last egg to prevent curdling.

Sift both flours into the bowl and gently fold in, adding just enough milk to give a mixture that drops slowly from a spoon when the spoon is held away from the bowl. Fold in the orange zest and orange flavouring.

Pour the batter into the prepared tin and bake for 30–40 minutes or until golden-brown on top and a skewer inserted into the centre comes out clean.

Turn the cake onto a cooling rack and leave to cool. Slice and enjoy.

TIPPŁES

THE FORTHCOMING

I have a son named Chase. He is eight years old now and although he doesn't care to tell us much about what he's thinking or feeling, I'm seeing glimpses of his personality from new angles every day. One thing about Chase is that once he sets his mind on something he does not let go, and I'll hear about the same thing day and night. Despite it being mildly irritating, there is something to admire about that tenacity. It's something too many of us lose when we grow older. These days I turn on the news and find that 'change' is a frequent topic. It's clear to us, as a global community, that we must collectively work together for a better tomorrow. For all our sakes.

However, this 'change' is a funny, elusive sort of thing. The idea of change is easily seen but what we deem as actual change, something that is satisfactory, is much more difficult to find. Perhaps there is something philosophical in this, perhaps humanity will never be satisfied, perhaps the utopia that we wish to find cannot ever really exist. Still, is this an excuse not to try? I won't be the first and I will definitely not be the last person to learn from an eight-year-old. Of course, the things Chase decides to persist on are much less logical. I understand the desire to make a difference to the world and the desire to eat another doughnut, even though you are so full up from the last one that you might be sick, are two different matters. However, the important things here are passion, perseverance and drive.

Although Sierra Leone is very beautiful and gifted with many natural resources, it is not the terrestrial paradise it once was to our ancestors who took refuge in its forest and mountains. Ironically, today's Sierra Leone has become more of a prison to most of the population and a playground to the elite who are able to live there. This is caused by many factors: war, corruption and exploitation, mixed with a plethora of other uncontrollable factors such as natural disasters and the effects of climate change. There are so many factors that it is hard to determine any one reason why Sierra Leone has ended up this way. When so much is out of our hands, we can only pick up the pieces bit by bit to build the Sierra Leone that we wish to see and know exists. With our ambitions kept close to heart, we can choose to move forward.

There is a certain wonder in knowing that, unless you tear down the mountains and bulldoze the land, Sierra Leone can never truly have nothing. They say that 'in times of great struggle, nature provides' and I believe our greatest failing point has been underestimating this belief. The biodiversity of Sierra Leone is truly one of kind. According to the Convention on Biological Diversity around 15,000 plant species have been identified as well as 170 mammal species, 274 bird species (14 of which are endangered) and there are about 213 fish species that have been discovered so far.

I IMAGINE A FUTURE IN SIERRA LEONE IN WHICH OUR LANDSCAPE IS FULL OF FLOWERS AND ALIVE WITH BIRDSONG.

It is also notable that Sierra Leone is home to 15 species of primate, all of which are endangered or vulnerable, making the country a conservationist's dream. Although it may sound crude to put conservation and profit in the same sentence, this is something I truly hope that Sierra Leone may one day achieve. In knowing that our country is a golden chest of treasures, I see a time in the future where Sierra Leone can profit off the land sustainably, using tourism instead of stopgap methods that keep us trapped in poverty, filling the pockets of the few, while overrunning the land that has nurtured us.

If there is any organisation that understands this, it has to be Tacugama Chimpanzee Sanctuary. They have been doing conservation work in Sierra Leone since their founder, Bala Amarasekaran and his wife Sharmila, rescued a chimp from what could have been a very grim and gloomy future, as he was being sold on the side of the road in 1988.

Besides protecting Sierra Leone's chimps, Tacugama does work to support the local communities and is one of Sierra Leone's greatest tourist spots. So, why stop at chimps? I imagine a future in Sierra Leone in which our landscape is full of flowers and alive with birdsong. Wherever you are, you will be able to see and hear wildlife nearby, and know that even the most rare, threatened and endangered species have populations that are stable,

resilient and recovering. I understand that this will not be easy; preventing species extinction is an enormous challenge and depends on a sound understanding of the complex interdependencies between people and nature. But it is not impossible, and this is the most important message I could give.

A country's diaspora, and the diasporas it hosts, can be a huge asset for its development. We are a channel through which not only money, but also much tacit knowledge, can flow. We are a potential source of opportunities for trade, investment, innovation and professional networks. Governments should have a diaspora strategy that builds on natural feelings of identity and affection to cultivate this social network as a powerful source of economic progress. If we want to harness the value that is under our noses, we can do much more to raise the importance of environmental awareness with our government and other stakeholders, we can raise awareness of the depth and breadth of wildlife, flora and fauna we are blessed with and the eco-tourism potential it holds. We can all become ambassadors for our cherished Tacugama and the great work they have been dedicated to for decades, because if they thrive, we thrive.

Conservation offers a long-term solution to many of the country's issues. However, in the short term, desperate measures are needed to solve more desperate issues. Sierra Leone is

listed as the 13th poorest country in the world according to World Bank data from 2020; the amount of money trickling down to the common folk is unbelievably small and it is due to extreme poverty that crime rates are high, and the quality of life is low. Action on Poverty (ATP) is an organisation that works in Sierra Leone and other countries to provide support that goes beyond simple donations to individuals, as this does not attack the root of the problem. Instead, they help people grow their own livelihoods by sharing business skills with them. After attending one of APT's baking apprenticeships, Abie, from Moyamba in Sierra Leone's Southern Province, commented on how this charity has affected her life: 'My monthly income before acquiring the skills was 25,000 Leones and today it is 265,000. I feel very proud of my contributions to household income.'

I truly believe that these two charities have the potential to make a real difference to Sierra Leone. They are not the solution to all of Sierra Leone's problems but will help tackle a few of them. Change is driven by the heart's ambition and is realised by our actions. It's not that the 'satisfactory change' we seek does not exist but that we are not patient enough to see it through. I'll put it this way: small steps in the right direction are better than big steps the wrong direction. With perseverance, we'll get there eventually.

NOMOLI TIKI

50ml (1³⁄₄oz) nomoli

50ml (1³⁄₄oz) gold rum, such as Appleton signature blend

15ml (¹⁄₂oz) lime juice

15ml (¹⁄₂oz) Chambord

TO GARNISH

mint sprig

fresh ginger slices

Put all the ingredients in a cocktail shaker filled with ice and shake for 30 seconds.

Strain into an ice-filled tiki glass.

Garnish with the mint sprig and ginger and serve.

Note: You can use brandy instead of gold rum, if you prefer.

MARIA'S MOJITO

5 lime wedges

5 blackberries

8 mint leaves

40ml (1¼oz) Shwen Purple Haze (lavender and coconut water)

soda water (club soda), to top up

mint sprig, to garnish

Muddle lime wedges, blackberries and mint leaves in a small jug, crushing the mint leaves and berries as you go. Pour into an ice-filled Collins glass and pour over the Purple Haze lavender and coconut water, stirring with a long-handled spoon. Top up with soda water and garnish with mint sprig to serve.

LEONE STAR (NAMED AFTER THE SIERRA LEONE NATIONAL FOOTBALL TEAM)

30ml (1oz) Pineapple and Star Fruit Juice
(see below)

30ml (1oz) gin

15ml (½ oz) lime juice

20–30ml (½–1oz) Honey Syrup (see below)

chilled prosecco, to top up

star fruit slice, to garnish

> Pour the Pineapple and Star Fruit Juice into an ice-filled cocktail shaker with the gin, lime juice and Honey Syrup.
>
> Shake and pour into a coupe glass. Top with prosecco, garnish with star fruit and serve.

PINEAPPLE AND STAR FRUIT JUICE

½ pineapple, peeled and chopped

2 star fruit, chopped

Put the pineapple and star fruit in a juicer and process to a juice following the manufacturer's instructions. Pour into a large jug and set aside in the fridge until needed (use within 2 days).

HONEY SYRUP

85g (2¾oz) honey

60ml (2oz) water

Combine the ingredient in a small pan over medium heat and simmer, stirring, for 5 minutes. Cool completely before use. The honey syrup will keep for up to 1 month stored in a clean airtight container in the fridge.

TOMBE SOUR

1 egg white (or 1 tbsp pasteurized egg white)

60ml (2oz) bourbon

30ml (1oz) lemon juice

40ml (1¼oz) Shwen Tombe (tamarind juice)

15ml (½oz) maple syrup

TO GARNISH

twist of lemon zest

dash of Angostura bitters

Put the egg white in a small bowl and use a whisk to whisk until frothy, 2–3 minutes. (You will only need a dash of egg white for this recipe.)

Put all of the ingredients into a cocktail shaker filled with ice cubes. Shake well until the outside of the shaker feels cold. Pour into a coupe glass, garnish and serve.

Note: Consuming raw eggs comes with a risk of salmonella. We recommend using pasteurized egg white for this recipe.

GINGER SPICED SOUR

30ml (1oz) Shwen Nomoli ginger beer

30ml (1oz) Disaronno amaretto liqueur

10ml (⅓oz) lemon juice

15ml (½oz) lime juice

dash of clove syrup

small piece of preserved (candied) ginger or 1 cinnamon stick, to serve

Put all the ingredients in a cocktail shaker filled with ice and shake for 30 seconds. Strain into a tumbler, adding extra ice if required.

Garnish with preserved (candied) ginger or a cinnamon stick to serve.

MAN, GO ENJOY THE SUNSHINE!

60ml (2oz) cachaça

22.5ml (¾oz) Lillet Blanc

15ml (½oz) lime juice

Shwen Mango Sunshine lemonade, to top up

half a grapefruit slice, to garnish

Put all the ingredients, apart from the Mango Sunshine lemonade, into a cocktail shaker. Shake well and strain into an ice-filled Collins glass.

Top with Mango Sunshine mango lemonade and garnish with the grapefruit slice.

GINGER AND PINEAPPLE BLAST

75ml (2¼oz) pineapple juice

15ml (½oz) lime juice

1–2 dashes grenadine

Shwen Nomoli ginger beer

lime wedge, to garnish

Pour the pineapple juice and lime juice into a cocktail shaker filled with ice, add the grenadine and shake until the outside of the shaker feels really cold.

Pour the cocktail mixture into a Collins glass filled with ice, then top up with the Shwen Nomoli ginger beer.

Garnish with a lime wedge and serve.

SERVES 1

MALVACAEA SPRITZ

I named this cocktail after a family of flowering plants that includes the mallow and hibiscus. It has a beautiful floral colour.

Grape syrup is a widely available condiment made with concentrated grape juice. It is thick and sweet because of its high ratio of sugar to water, and is widely available online.

50ml (1¾oz) Shwen Spiced Bissap ginger and hibiscus juice

50ml (1¾oz) grapefruit juice

15ml (½oz) lime juice

10ml (⅓oz) grape syrup

soda water (club soda), to top up

TO GARNISH

grapefruit zest or peel

thin slice fresh ginger

Pour the Shwen Spiced Bissap ginger and hibiscus juice, grapefruit juice, lime juice and grape syrup into a cocktail shaker filled with ice and shake until the outside of the shaker feels really cold.

Pour the cocktail mixture into a Collins glass filled with ice, then top up with the soda water. Garnish with the grapefruit and ginger and serve.

PURPLE PICADOR

40ml (1¼oz) mezcal

20ml (½oz) kumquat liqueur

20ml (½oz) lime juice

30ml (1oz) Shwen Purple Haze lavender
and coconut water

dash of agave syrup

TO GARNISH

salt

lime wedge

Pour all of the ingredients into a mixing glass filled with ice cubes. Stir well and strain into a chilled Martini glass. Serve straight or on the rocks, sprinkle the salt over the drink and garnish with the lime wedge.

SERVES 1

G&T (GRAPE AND TAMARIND)

8 mint leaves

12.5ml (¼oz) lemon juice

50ml (1¾oz) Shwen Tombe tamarind juice

50ml (1¾oz) grape juice

TO GARNISH

a few mint leaves

3–4 grapes

Muddle the mint leaves and lemon juice in a cocktail shaker. Add the Shwen Tombe tamarind juice and grape juice. Fill with ice and shake for 10–12 seconds or until shaker feels cold outside.

Skewer the mint leaves and grapes alternately on a wooden skewer.

Strain the cocktail into an ice-filled Collins glass, garnish and serve.

FROM THE GARDENS OF SIERRA LEONE

A nomoli is a carved stone figurine native to Sierra Leone and Liberia. They are usually made of soapstone, limestone or granite and this colour is similar to that of my fiery ginger beer.

The nomoli figurines were used for protection and thought to have health benefits, just like my ginger beer.

3 cucumber slices

8 mint leaves

22.5ml (¾oz) lime juice

10ml (⅓oz) sugar syrup

15ml (½oz) Velvet Falernum liqueur

45ml (1½oz) Cognac

Shwen Nomoli ginger beer, to top up

TO GARNISH

cucumber slice

mint sprig

Muddle the cucumber slices, mint leaves, lime juice, sugar syrup and Velvet Falernum in a cocktail shaker.

Add the Cognac, fill with ice and shake for 10–12 seconds. Strain into a Collins glass filled with ice, top up with Shwen Nomoli ginger beer, garnish and serve.

WEST AFRICAN BUCK

25ml (½oz) lemon juice

1 ripe strawberry

10ml (⅓oz) sugar syrup

2 dashes of Angostura bitters

60ml (1oz) gin

Shwen Spiced Bissap (ginger and hibiscus juice), to top up

TO GARNISH

fresh hibiscus petals

fresh ginger slices

Muddle the lemon juice, strawberry, syrup and bitters in a cocktail shaker filled with ice. Add the gin and shake for 10–12 seconds.

Strain into a Collins glass filled with ice. Top up with the Shwen Spiced Bissap ginger and hibiscus juice. Garnish with the hibiscus and ginger and serve.

Note: Vodka and bourbon also work well in place of the gin.

TIME FOR FRUIT TEA!

Hibiscus powder is available online or from most health food shops. It is a 100 per cent natural powder made from the nutrient-rich red petals of the hibiscus calyx.

50ml (1¾oz) Shwen Passionately Bissap juice

20ml (½oz) lime juice

dash of honey

ginger kombucha, to top up

TO SUGAR THE RIM

caster sugar

hibiscus powder

Pour the Shwen Passionately Bissap juice, lime juice and a dash of honey into a cocktail shaker filled with ice and shake until the outside of the shaker feels really cold.

To sugar the rim, mix the sugar and hibiscus powder in a shallow plate. Moisten the rim of the glass with a little water, then gently upturn the glass and coat the rim with the hibiscus and sugar powder.

Fill the sugared glass with ice, pour in the cocktail mixture, then top up with ginger kombucha and serve.

AFRICAN NEGRONI

30ml (1oz) London dry gin

30ml (1oz) Campari

30ml (1oz) Shwen Passionately Bissap hibiscus
and strawberry juice, to top up

orange twist, to garnish

Stir all of the ingredients together in a mixing glass filled with ice until well
chilled. Strain into a rocks glass filled with ice, garnish and serve.

SERVES 1

HIBISCUS BREAKFAST MARTINI

50ml (1¾oz) Shwen Spiced Bissap ginger
and hibiscus juice, to top up

20ml (½oz) Triple Sec

30ml (1oz) gin

1 tbsp hibiscus jam (you can find hibiscus
jam online)

fresh hibiscus petals, to serve

Combine all of the ingredients in a cocktail shaker filled with ice.
Shake until well chilled. Double strain into a coupe glass and garnish
with hibiscus petals to serve.

THE PROCESS OF MAKING OGIRIE, CASSAVA BREAD AND PALM OIL

OGIRIE

On our trip, we travelled to the small coastal village of York and met Aba Mensah, who showed us how ogirie is traditionally made. Ogirie is a paste made of fermented sesame seeds and, much like miso, it is used as a flavouring. The process of making it is very labour-intensive. First, the sesame seeds need to be de-husked, which is traditionally done using a large wooden pestle and mortar. Aba stressed the importance of removing all the outer shells of the seeds, because if it's not done properly, then you risk wasting all your hard work and ending up with bitter ogirie.

I could see that this took a lot of arm strength, and I even began to feel tired just watching! Then the seeds were washed and the leftover husk was used to feed the chickens. After this, the seeds are put into a large pot, placed on top of the stove and left to boil for hours. Aba explained to me that after it is finished boiling, the ogirie is wrapped in a burlap sack and left to ferment for a few days, and – after what would feel like decades of waiting – it's removed from the sack, pounded with a pestle and mortar then wrapped in banana leaves and smoked. Smoking does two things: kills bacteria and adds flavour.

While this process was being explained and demonstrated by Aba, her two close friends and work partners, Abigail Coker and Nancy Gbono,

were by her side ready to help. It was clear that the two of them had a lot of respect for Aba. Although they seemed close, like sisters, she was revered for her skill and throughout the process they would frequently check things by her.

CASSAVA BREAD

At Waterloo, in the Western Area of Sierra Leone, we met Ramatu Kamara, whose business selling cassava bread had become her only source of income after losing her husband. Ramatu proudly mentioned to me that her recipe for cassava bread had been in her family for generations; it had been passed down to her from her mother, and her mother had learned it from her mother before her, and so on and so forth.

Other than her incredible strength of character, one thing I admired about Ramatu was her generosity and kindness: her cassava bread was so popular that she was selling it wholesale, but, rather than keeping this recipe to herself, she was providing classes for women in the community so that they could also learn to make and sell cassava bread to support their families. And solely from selling her cassava bread, Ramatu has been able to build a house for herself and her children.

When we went to Ramatu's shop, although they had just got back from school, her children were all helping out. In the West, they might be

IT'S UNDENIABLE THAT SIERRA LEONEAN WOMEN ARE A FORCE TO BE RECKONED WITH.

seen as outstandingly well-behaved, but in Sierra Leone the reality that the family business puts food on your table and pays your school fees is a little more real. Knowing this, you learn to treasure your parents' work even more. Seeing them reminded me slightly of my childhood and even listening to Ramatu's story felt familiar as I recalled my great-grandmother's plight. It's undeniable that Sierra Leonean women are a force to be reckoned with.

RED PALM OIL

Red palm oil is native to West Africa and has remained a vital part of our culture, livelihoods and cuisine for over 5,000 years. Red palm oil is a staple not only in Sierra Leone but throughout West Africa. This shiny red oil with its smoky flavour gives the stamp of authenticity to West African cuisine. It's virtually impossible to replicate that flavour. In Sierra Leone, artisanal production of this red liquid gold is controlled primarily by rural women.

In 2009 a study was published in the British Journal of Biomedical Science that found consumption of red palm oil may reduce cholesterol levels and help protect the heart and immune system. We feel the same way about our red palm oil the way Italians and others around the Mediterranean feel about olive oil. As with any type of fat, palm oil should be consumed in moderation.

Palm oil is one of those quintessentially West African flavours. It has a rich, earthy and slightly nutty taste, adding serious depth to any pot of stew, beans or pottage, even elevating a humble boiled yam (another star ingredient in its own right!) with its complex aromas. Its bright red colour comes from the high concentration of beta carotene (used by the body to make Vitamin A) and lycopene, the latter of which may have some health benefits. However, this vegetable oil, similarly to coconut oil, contains high levels of saturated fat and, when consumed in excess, can harm cardiovascular health.

In a process taking several days, tappers climb oil palm trees (*Elaeis guineensis*) to incredible heights to release the palm fruits, which are then left to ripen until the nuts within can easily be dislodged from their husks. The nuts are cooked until soft, then pressed underfoot and rinsed to draw out the oil. Produced this way, it is sustainable both environmentally and economically. For the recipes in this book, always use red palm oil, preferably from Sierra Leone; the finest in all of West Africa.

Oil palm trees are native to Africa and historically grew in West Africa and, during the late 19th and early 20th centuries, they were introduced to Indonesia and Malaysia. Please be sure to source sustainable palm oil; this means palm oil that's used and produced in a way that doesn't harm the environment by damaging rain forests and degrading the natural habitat for wildlife.

HE WOULD TREAD ON PALM KERNELS FOR HOURS AND HOURS, AND AS A RESULT HE WAS PROBABLY ONE OF THE STRONGEST PEOPLE I HAD EVER MET.

When we arrived at the town of Bo on our trip, we met Agifa Luseni, who took us to his farm and showed us the process of making palm oil the traditional way. He would tread on palm kernels for hours and hours, and as a result he was probably one of the strongest people I had ever met. He was very friendly and eager to show us his work; nothing was too difficult for him. Agifa's farm produced not only palm oil but also peanuts and pineapples. There were coconut trees too – we were able to catch another glimpse of Agifa's superhuman strength as he scaled one of the coconut trees to grab us something to drink!

As we walked through the pineapple farm, I recalled a story that I had heard about snakes in pineapple farms. As my nerves heightened, I couldn't help but ask Agifa if there would likely be snakes and, much to my displeasure, he said there definitely would be snakes. I quickly realised that I had made a grave mistake by revealing my fear to everybody, as they all rushed to pick up branches and leaves to drag across my legs.

It worked every time, and thinking back, I believe everyone has me to thank for not seeing any snakes, as I probably scared them off with all the screaming. Having said that, I tasted one of the best pineapples I've ever had in my life at Agifa's farm, and given the chance to try his fruit again, I would definitely take the risk of being bitten by a snake.

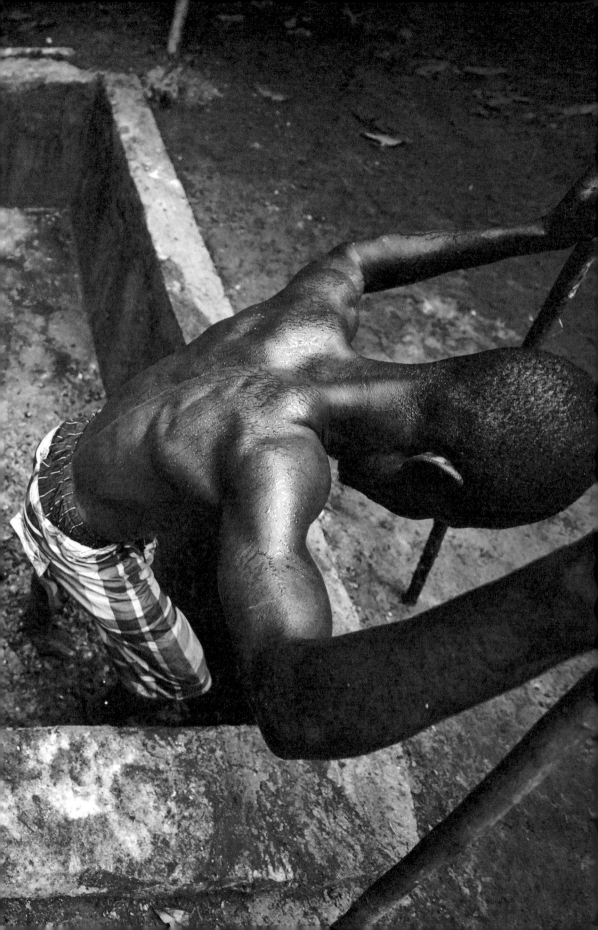

GLOSSARY

Bitter leaves/bittas/processed frozen bitter leaves (see Bitter Leaf and Bologie, page 161)

The botanical name for bittas is *Vernonia amygdalina*. It is a leafy shrub or small tree that grows in tropical Africa that can reach up to 6m (20ft) when fully grown. (Fun fact: it's actually a member of the daisy family!) True to its name, bittas is very bitter. Usually sold frozen, these leaves contain many vitamins and are said to have antibacterial properties.

Before cooking with the leaves, you have to first wash them thoroughly by rubbing them together under running water. Taste to try it first to check before adding it – you want just a slightly bitter taste.

Bor-boueh seeds (see Bor-boueh Sauce, page 156)

Bor-boueh (known as ogbono in Nigeria) seeds come from the fruit of trees in the Irvingia genus of African and South East Asian trees. It is also known by the common names wild mango, African mango, bush mango, dika or mbukpap uyo. The edible mango-like fruits and are especially valued for their fat- and protein-rich seeds and are used to thicken soups and stews. They are sold as whole seeds.

Calabash nutmeg (or African nutmeg) (see Yam Pancakes with Smoked Mackerel and Horseradish Cream, page 69)

Calabash nutmeg (*Monodora myristica Dunal*) is the dried seed from a tropical forest tree native to West Africa. Like many spices, it has several names. You may have come across it as African or Jamaican nutmeg, or know it in a Nigerian tongue as airama, ehuru (Igbo), ariwo (Yoruba), iwo (Erhe), lubushi, ehiri or airama. Other names include ehu and muscadier de calabash. It is also called ehuru, ehu, ariwo, awerewa, ehiri, airama, African nutmeg or Jamaican nutmeg.

It comes from evergreen forests of West Africa, specifically from the tropical tree *Monodora myristica*. It was introduced to Jamaica and parts of the Caribbean in the 18th century during the slave trade. You must only use a tiny bit because it is potent, with a taste similar to ordinary nutmeg, although the two plants are not closely realated. It is sold whole and can be grated or ground in a spice grinder.

Cassava

Cassava (*Manihot esculenta*) is a tuber with a waxy, bark-like outer skin and a starchy centre. It was introduced into Sierra Leone (and Africa more broadly) by Portuguese traders between 1415 and 1600 when they dominated world trade. It is now cultivated in more than 40 countries across the continent. It's also known in other countries as manioc and yuca, and is widely grown worldwide.

Cassava is one of the major staple foods for Sierra Leoneans, second to rice. For many people in major cassava production districts of the country, it is the major staple. The most popular meal made from it is Garri Eba (see page 160), which is common in many West African countries. It can also be used to make Cassava Flatbread (see page 124). It's sold fresh in supermarkets and Afro-Caribbean shops.

Note: Cassava should not be eaten raw in large quantities because it contains a naturally occurring cyanide that is toxic to humans. Soaking, fermenting and cooking cassava are processes that render the toxin harmless.

Cocoyam (see Ebbeh with Cured Mackerel, page 119)

Cocoyam (or taro) is a nutritious root vegetable that is eaten across the African continent. Growing up to 1.8m (6ft) tall, cocoyam is a large perennial plant with heart-shaped leaves and turnip-sized corms (the edible part). Beneath the skin, the colour of its flesh varies from white to cream to yellow or purple, and it has water chestnut-like nutty flavour.

Sold fresh, it shouldn't be eaten raw – treat it as you would a potato or sweet potato. You can soak cocoyam in water when it's peeled, to avoid discolouration.

Cubeb pepper (see West African Pepper Blend, page 23)

Sometimes called Java Pepper because of its Indonesian origin. Cubeb reached Africa by way of Arab traders. It is similar in appearance to black pepper but has its stalks attached. It has a mild peppery flavour with a slight bitter aftertaste, and is sold dried.

Drinks

You can easily replace the Shwen Shwen juices in the Tipples chapter with juices of similar flavours, if you'd prefer to – although you may find the result isn't quite as delicious!

Egusi seeds

Egusi (also known by variations, including agusi, agushi) is the name for the fat- and protein-rich seeds of certain cucurbitaceous plants (squash, melon, gourd) which, after being dried and ground, are used as a major ingredient in West African cuisine.

There's a bit of disagreement on whether the word is used more properly to describe the seeds of the colocynth (*Citrullus colocynthis*), those of a particular large-seeded variety of watermelon, or generically for the seeds of any cucurbitaceous plant. The characteristics and uses of all these seeds are broadly similar. Major egusi-growing nations include Mali, Burkina Faso, Togo, Ghana, Côte d'Ivoire, Benin, Nigeria and Cameroon.

Fonio and fonio flour

Fonio is made from an ancient African grain. It's cultivated from two species of grass with small grains, is drought-tolerant and can be grown year-round. It's extremely nutritious with a very favourable taste. It's gluten free and high in dietary fibre. The grains can be used to make porridge, bread and beer and it can be made into flour as well.

Garri (see Garri Eba, page 160)

Garri – dried, toasted, granulated cassava – is made from the dried, ground tuberous roots of the cassava plant (see opposite). The dried granules have a texture similar to medium semolina. Garri is a major part of the diet among various ethnicities of Nigeria, Benin Republic, Togo, Ghana, Guinea, Cameroon, Sierra Leone and Liberia.

Grains of paradise (see West African Pepper Blend, page 23)

Grains of paradise are seeds from the *Aframomum melegueta* plant. This aromatic spice has an appearance similar to peppercorns but their origin is firmly in West Africa. With notes of cardamom, coriander, citrus, ginger, nutmeg and juniper, they pack a light peppery heat. Also known as melegueta pepper, guinea grains and guinea pepper.

Grains of selim (see Kankankan Spice Mix, page 56)

Grains of selim (*Xylopia aethiopica*), sold dried like pepper corns, are also known as selim pepper, uda, Ethiopian pepper, Guinea pepper and Kani pepper. The pods come from a tree that can grow up to 20m (65ft) high and is native to the lowland rainforest and most fringe forests in the savanna zones of Africa.

Hibiscus/Roselle (see Cured and Blow-torched Mackerel with Hibiscus and Ginger Sauce, page 54)

Roselle (*Hibiscus sabdariffa*) is a species of flowering plant native to West Africa. In the 16th and early 17th centuries it was taken to the West Indies and Asia respectively, where it has since become naturalised in many places. Two main types are available: red petals and white petals. In Sierra Leone we mainly use red petals to make tea and soft drinks, while white roselle is use in savoury dishes. Both petals have a similar flavour.

The white petals are steamed, packaged and frozen. To use them, you just need to rinse them first; any you don't use can be stored in the freezer for up to two months. As with beetroot, handle the dried red petals with caution, as their intense colour can stain!

Jakato (see Jakato Fritters with Spicy Tomato Sauce, page 71)

Bitter balls, garden eggs or jakato as it is commonly known in Freetown, is a fruit from the African garden aubergine (eggplant) called *Solanum aethiopicum*. Sold fresh, like aubergine, it is low in sodium, low in calories and very high in dietary fibre. A slightly sweet, tender fruit covered with a shiny skin, it is often used in savoury dishes.

Jute leaves/krain krain (see Krain Krain, page 146)

Jute leaves are sold in African shops and in some supermarkets (often frozen), usually in 400g (14oz) packages. The fresh leaves are destemmed, cut finely and cooked in a base sauce. Its texture is intentionally, and pleasantly, slimy. They are very similar in consistency when cooked to okra.

When harvested young, the leaves are generally flavourful and tender; older leaves tend to be fibrous and woody. Jute leaves are not just for culinary uses but are also known for their medicinal properties and are used to make rope, paper and other products.

Moringa powder (see Moringa Ice Cream, page 192)

Moringa oleifera is a plant that is often called the drumstick tree, the miracle tree, the ben oil tree, or the horseradish tree. It tastes like matcha that has been spiked with notes of spirulina-like blue-green algae. The powder dissolves easily in water, providing a distinctly 'green' flavour that is bitter and slightly sweet. In Sierra Leone, fresh moringa leaves are used to make a kind of tea and in savoury dishes.

Ogirie (fermented sesame seeds)

The sesame plant is native to West and Central Africa and was cultivated before written history. It's an important plant in Sierra Leone: the seeds are often used to facilitate childbirth, heal sprains and as topical remedy to heal stings of scorpions. Sesame seeds are also used fermented to make our staple seasoning, ogiri.

Once opened, ogirie can be stored for a long time, or kept frozen. It's easy to buy frozen, but is usually used fresh in Sierra Leone. Ogirie adds a salty, savoury flavour to dishes (similar to miso). To make ogirie, the seeds are first boiled, then left to ferment. Salt is added and then it's smoked (see page 233).

Palm butter/cream (see Chicken Suprêmes in Palm Butter Sauce, page 106)

Many African recipes call for the fruit and oil of the African oil palm (*Elaesis guineensis*). Palm butter is made by boiling and grinding the palm fruit (palm nuts). It is a labour of love and requires time. Most cooks in the UK use ready-prepared tinned palm butter (also sold as palm cream or palm nut concentrate).

To prepare tinned palm butter for cooking, I empty the contents of the tin into a large bowl, add 1 litre (35fl oz/4⅓ cups) of hot water and then mix and strain the mixture through a sieve (strainer) several times to remove any chaff that remains from the pounded palm nuts. The resulting liquid is then used for cooking. It has a rich red colour and gives a silky, buttery richness to cooked dishes. Be careful cooking with it, as it can stain.

Plantains

Plantains are a member of the banana family, but they are starchy, not sweet. These fruits can be green, yellow or almost black, according to how ripe they are. Plantain is a staple food in Africa, and they are mostly grown in small-scale compound gardens. West Africa is one of the main plantain-producing regions of the world.

Cooked plantains are nutritionally very similar to a potato, calorie-wise, but contain more of some vitamins and minerals.

Red palm oil

Palm oil has a rich, earthy and slightly nutty taste, adding a lovely depth to any dish with its complex aromas. Its bright red colour comes from the high concentration of beta carotene and lycopenes.

Once opened, palm oil keeps for a long time

if stored in a cool, dark place. Like coconut oil, it will set solid in colder weather. If this happens, just melt it before use.

Palm oil has an intense colour, so be careful as it does stain (see page 236).

Sawa sawa/sour leaf/gongura leaves

Sawa sawa leaves are used to impart a tart flavour to dishes. It comes in two varieties: one with a red stem (which has a more sour flavour) and one with a green stem. We tend to use the green-stem variety.

Sweet tamarind (see Black Velvet Tamarind Sorbet, page 200)

Sweet tamarind is the fruit of the *Tamarindus indica*, from the Fabaceae family, which is indigenous to Africa. The fruits have a hard, velvety black shell, orange sticky pulp and flat circular brown seeds (the shell and seeds are not eaten). It is very popular with children, time-consuming to peel but popular because it is sweet. It is sold dried in bags, and already peeled.

Alternatives: Black Velvet Tamarind/Black Tomblah. Black tomblah is usually available early in the year, in January to March, but Sweet Tamarind is available year-round, and online.

Smoked fish fillets

Smoking fish as a method of preservation has been used for at least 5,000 years in Africa and it remains a staple food product and source of income for many African coastal communities. In the tropical conditions, fresh fish spoils quickly and refrigeration isn't commonplace. Techniques such as sun-drying, salting, fermenting and smoking allow fish to be stored for months, even years.

Local fishermen bring their catch to the beach – catfish, herring, mackerel, or whatever is caught that day. The fish is gutted and taken home, ready to be smoked in the traditional way. Metal drums or mud stoves are loaded with firewood to produce smoke, over which the fish are placed in a metal grill.

The omega-3 fatty acids have recognised health benefits. Dried fish also is a fantastic source of protein and is appreciated for the umami flavour it imparts to food. In Sierra Leone and across West Africa, we love that umami flavour and it can be found in so many of our dishes, from soups to stews. Dried fish can be stewed, steamed or boiled and used as a flavour enhancer.

Dried bonga fillets are particularly popular with Sierra Leonean cooks and in my recipes, dried bonga fillets or smoked dried snapper should ideally be used. These can be substituted with dried anchovies (or even dried mackerel, but be aware that this will bring an extra saltiness to the dish). If you are using anchovies, make sure to soak them for about 30 minutes and rinse a couple of times with fresh clean water to get rid of the salt.

Tola powder (see Tola Sauce, page 154)

The tola tree (*Beilschmiedia mannii*) is native to the rainforests of Sierra Leone. It is a small evergreen tree that can reach up to 10m (33ft) in height. In Sierra Leone, there are many traditional recipes using the flowers, leaves and especially the seeds of this plant. The fruit is a berry with a thin skin that turns red when it reaches maturity, with a seed inside. It blooms in January and bears fruit between October and December. To the local communities, the tola is an important source of income, especially for its wood (commercial names are kanda and kanda rosa), used to produce window fixtures, furniture, floors, canoes, etc, often as a substitute for mahogany.

The dried seeds and the powder made from them are rich in protein, carbohydrates, calcium and phosphorus. They are used to thicken soups, and we also use them to thicken other leafy vegetable stew dishes in Sierra Leone. Tola has delicious savoury, earthy tones combined with a nutty, even fruity flavour that it retains even when cooked.

Wallah rice (see Pemahun, page 158)

This is our very own 'wallah res', which is chunky and with a very nice texture. Wallah is a chiefdom in Kambia district in the Northern Province of Sierra Leone, where there is fertile soil for rice cultivation. Rice cultivation in West Africa has an extensive and rich history, dating back to around 3,500 years ago, when Africans living in the tropical regions began growing rice in this part of Africa.

Yams

Yams are a starchy edible root of the Dioscorea genus and are used in many African dishes and are very popular in African cooking. Yams should not be confused with sweet potatoes. They have a white flesh and a texture that is similar to a turnip. The flesh can be eaten boiled, roasted, baked, mashed or made into chips.

STOCKISTS

Most of these ingredients are widely available in African shops and, increasingly, in supermarkets and online (from websites such as Amazon and Ebay and from specialist food suppliers).

If you do go into an African food shop, you will find that the owners will always want to help you and will been keen to track down what you need!

I also keep an updated list on my website of stockists by country, and city.

Visit **shwenshwen.com**

SOURCES

Dedication

evaw-global-database.unwomen.org/en/countries/africa/sierra-leone

A Brief History Of Sierra Leone, pages 13–17

www.newworldencyclopedia.org/entry/Sahel

en.wikisource.org/wiki/1911_Encyclop%C3%A6dia_Britannica/ Fernandez,_Alvaro

www.britannica.com/place/western-Africa/The-slave-trade-era

www.maggs.com/history-of-the-sierra-leone-battalion-of-the-royal-west-african-frontier-force_227638.htm

blogs.lse.ac.uk/africaatlse/2020/06/27/british-founding-sierra-leone-slave-trade/

Why Afro-Fusion Cooking Resonates with Me, pages 91–93

www.historyworld.net/wrldhis/plaintexthistories.asp?historyid=ad45

Returning To Sierra Leone, pages 181–182

www.ncbi.nlm.nih.gov/pmc/articles/PMC3842857/

The Forthcoming, pages 211–213

www.cbd.int/countries/profile/?country=sl

www.atlasandboots.com/travel-blog/poorest-countries-in-the-world-ranked/

aptuk.org.uk/about-us/

Red Palm Oil, pages 236–239

www.tandfonline.com/doi/abs/10.1080/09674845.2009.1173027

NOTES

- I use full fat milk unless stated otherwise.
- I use large free-range eggs
- Butter is salted unless stated otherwise

ACKNOWLEDGEMENTS

When I say that in Sierra Leone there is adventure around every corner, I could not mean it in a more literal sense. Before my recent trip, I was worried that I would not be able to capture everything I wanted to in the short period of time I had. Now I realise that, even without a structured itinerary, I would have been able to find the Sierra Leone that I want to tell people about in this book. Why? Because beyond the news stories and stereotypes, the Sierra Leone that 'should be' already is. The next thing to focus on is what 'could be'. I met so many extraordinary people on my trip and with every journey I felt myself falling more and more in love with Sweet Salone. Our heritage is something to be proud of as the inheritors of such a country, such a culture. We have a duty to celebrate and preserve it.

I would like to say a few thank yous.

First, to my grandmother, Mariama Kabba, who is a strong, independent woman and an inspiration to me. To my mother, Fatmata Bintu Bawoh; I do not always get on with her, but I cannot deny that she can cook. I mean really cook, and that has had a massive impact on me. To my Aunty Sahadatu Jah, who has had my back, supported me, seen the journey and witnessed the struggle and injustices. Also to my late Aunty Marie Sesay, who was one of the first people in Sierra Leone who showed me that, with determination, you can do what you love. She was the only professional chef in Sierra Leone I knew, having studied at the YWCA to gain her independence. When I first came to England, all Aunty Marie Sesay wanted me to send her was cookbooks. Well, now she is mentioned in one and I wish she were still alive to see it.

Finally, to my dear friend Rosaline Thomas, my bestie who's been there for fun and laughter, when this has all become overwhelming and all a bit too much.

SIERRA LEONE CHARITIES

On a more serious note, I would like to thank Alimatu Dimonekene for teaching me about the complex and surprising history of FGM in Sierra Leone, which is, tragically, still customary in some parts of the country today. Alimatu is a pro-women's and girls' rights advocate, and the founder of A Girl at a Time in Sierra Leone. She is a tireless activist, working to end female genital mutilation and in support of the women and girls affected by this practice.

As I mentioned on page 212, the Tacugama Chimpanzee Sanctuary and Action on Poverty are doing wonderful work in Sierra Leone. If you're curious to find out more about these organisations, their websites are here:

www.tacugama.com

www.aptuk.org.uk

FAMBUL DEM!

To my husband Ben. He's incredible. Inspirational, supportive, entrepreneurial, and it was he who first mentioned the prospect of a Sierra Leonean cookbook when we were first married, almost 20 years ago. He noted down recipes and he made a booklet, which we still have. It was Ben who first imagined this book.

My daughter Charlie Yeanni is my little Shakespeare, my first port of call for copy-editing. She's great with written English and storytelling. My son Chase-man the space-man. Neurodiversity is part of our lives and, to Chase, the world can be complicated at times, difficult and stressful; but autism is a unique experience for everyone, totally intriguing and sometimes mysterious, which keeps me creative and is part of the reason why I love him so much.

Finally, to Rudi our giant schnauzer, who drives me around the bend.

TEAM DEM

I would like to thank Elise Dillsworth, my literary agent and fellow Sierra Leonean, for encouraging me to write this book. She's unflinchingly honest, fastidious. While my husband imagined it, it was Elise who persuaded me to do it. I would like to thank Sarah Lavelle at Quadrille Publishing for backing this endeavour, and commissioning editor Sarah Thickett for her patience and empathy. And Ade Daramy, for his valuable insights and for reading the history sections of this book.

For organising our amazing trip to Sierra Leone, I would like to thank Jacqueline Tschinkel from Hello Sierra Leone in Freetown. Jacky's team made us welcome and helped us at every stage: thank you Alusine Fab Fambulleh, Francis Momoh, our translator (who is also a public historian and cultural conservationist), and Ibrahim Barrie, our driver, who was strict but also fair, calm and gentle. He was the anchor of our group and kept us all together.

We also met many wonderful people during our stay, including Aba Mensah, Abigail Coker, Nancy Gbono, Ramatu Kamara, Agifa Luseni and many others.

David ('White boy snap-snap') Brown: taking someone to Sierra Leone for the first time can feel like when you introduce two close friends, it makes you nervous, and you desperately wish for them to get along. From when I first met David at the airport, he was excited and, knowing that he was looking forward to the trip, I did not want to disappoint him. Many of the shots Dave took were of ordinary people going through ordinary days but, by stealing a common moment from the graceless hands of time, it is made precious – Dave's stunning photography, designs and the cover for this book show that the real beauty of Sierra Leone is not only in its landscape, but also in its communities. Our heritage is something to be proud of and, as the heirs of such a country, such a culture, we have a duty to celebrate and preserve it.

I would like to thank Claire Rochford, head of design at Quadrille and Susan Low, our copy editor, who was exceptional when it comes to detail (and I like that), but, more than that, she took time to get to know me and my story. Finally, I would like to thank Yuki Sugiura, the most amazing food photographer, and food stylist Libby Silbermann, who it turns out is the queen of fufu. She deserves an honorary Sierra Leonean passport for that. Libby's wonderful team deserve a thank-you, too: Harriet Atkinson, Florence Blair and Sarah Vassallo, as well as Faye Wears, who sourced the beautiful props, and Kat Mead, who tested the recipes.

I couldn't have done it without you all.

INDEX

ABOUT THE AUTHOR

Maria Bradford grew up in Freetown, and started helping her mother prepare meals from about nine years old. Inspired by her heritage, Maria prepares traditional Sierra Leonean dishes and high-end Afro-fusion cuisine. Maria studied at Leith's School of Food and Wine and founded Maria Bradford Kitchen in 2017, which became known as Shwen Shwen. Her catering is in high demand for corporate events and private dining throughout the UK and Africa. Maria lives in the south of England with her husband and two children.

Managing Director
Sarah Lavelle

Commissioning Editor
Sarah Thickett

Head of Design
Claire Rochford

Design
Dave Brown

Recipe Photography
Yuki Sugiura

Location Photography
Dave Brown

Food Stylists
Libby Silbermann

Prop Stylist
Faye Wears

Head of Production
Stephen Lang

Production Controller
Gary Hayes

First published in 2023
by Quadrille, an imprint
of Hardie Grant Publishing

Quadrille
52–54 Southwark Street
London SE1 1UN
quadrille.com

Text © Maria Bradford 2023

Recipe Photography
© Yuki Sugiura 2023

Location Photography
© Dave Brown 2023

Design and layout
© Quadrille 2023

The cover was inspired by
country cloth (or Kpokpoi).
This thick, heavy cloth is a
traditional textile designed
with varying colours or stripes
used to make larger, more
complex patterns. Centuries
old, it originated within the
Mende / Sherbro tribes of Sierra
Leone and is woven on a drop
spindle using locally-sourced
raw cotton and ink from tree
bark. Traditionally worn by
Paramount Chiefs, it was seen
as a sign of wealth and prestige.

The rights of Maria Bradford
to be identified as the author
of this work have been asserted
by her in accordance with the
Copyright, Design and Patents
Act 1988.

Cataloguing in Publication Data:
a catalogue record for this book is
available from the British Library.

ISBN: 978 1 78713 796 7

Printed in China

FSC
www.fsc.org

MIX
Paper from
responsible sources
FSC™ C020056